Physical Characteristics of the Canaan Dog

(from the American Kennel Club

Body: Strong, displaying athletic agility and trimness.

Tail: Set moderately high. May be carried curled over the back when excited; limited to one full curl. When extended, the bone must reach to the hocks.

Coat: Double coat. Outer coat—straight, harsh, flat-lying, with slight ruff. Undercoat—straight, soft, short, flat-lying, density varying with climate.

Hindquarters: Moderately angulated. In balance with forequarters. Straight when viewed from the rear. Thigh musculature well developed, moderately broad. Hocks well let down. Dewclaws must be removed. Feet and nails as in forequarters.

Size: Height at the withers is 20 to 24 inches for dogs and 19 to 23 inches for bitches.

Feet: Catlike, pads hard, pigmentation harmonizing with nose and eye rims.

Canaan Dog

By Joy Levine

Contents

KENNEL CLUB BOOKS: **CANAAN DOG**
ISBN: 1-59378-349-3

Copyright © 2003 Kennel Club Books, Inc.
308 Main Street, Allenhurst, NJ 07711 USA
Cover Design Patented: US 6,435,559 B2 • Printed in South Korea

Photography by Carol Ann Johnson
with additional photographs by:

Norvia Behling, TJ Calhoun, Carolina Biological Supply, Doskocil, Isabelle Français, James Hayden-Yoav, James R Hayden, RBP, Bill Jonas, Dwight R Kuhn, Dr Dennis Kunkel, Mikki Pet Products, Phototake, Jean Claude Revy, Dr Andrew Spielman and Alice van Kempen.

Illustrations by Patricia Peters.

The publisher wishes to thank Richard and Ellen Minto and Myrna Shiboleth for allowing their dogs to be photographed for this book.

The Canaan Dog is an ancient member of the spitz family of dogs. Feral in nature but domesticated by dedicated fanciers, the Canaan Dog was originally used by the Israelites as herders and guard dogs; these are tasks that the breed still performs today.

HISTORY OF THE
CANAAN DOG

ORIGIN OF THE BREED

The Canaan Dog has an ancient and unique origin. The breed has been known since pre-biblical times, when they existed in the "Land of Canaan." In 2200–2000 BC, drawings and carvings of a dog that greatly resembles today's Canaan Dog appeared on the tombs of Beni-Hassan. The Canaan Dog was originally bred to guard and herd the camps and flocks of the Israelites. In the beginning, the breed was plentiful in the region until the scattering of Israelites by the Romans over 2,000 years ago. Once the Hebrew population decreased, a great deal of dogs sought new homes in the Negev Desert.

The Canaan Dog belongs to one of the oldest families of dog, the spitz family. Although many dogs throughout the Middle East are similar in appearance and temperament, the distinct Canaan Dog is found primarily in Israel. Dogs of similar type were also abundant in Egypt, Syria and the Sinai Desert. There are even some theories that purport that the Canaan Dog originated with the Indian Wolf. However, there is no

GENUS *CANIS*

Dogs and wolves are members of the genus *Canis*. Wolves are known scientifically as *Canis lupus* while dogs are known as *Canis domesticus*. Dogs and wolves are known to interbreed. The term "canine" derives from the Latin-derived word *Canis*. The term "dog" has no scientific basis but has been used for thousands of years. The origin of the word "dog" has never been authoritatively ascertained.

accurate proof that this theory is true.

The breed is basically a feral dog (semi-wild evolved through Natural Selection) that has been ushered into domestication. The term "feral" essentially means a once-domesticated animal that slips back into the wild. The Australian Dingo is a good example of a feral animal, as well as the Carolina Dog of the American South and the New Guinea Singing Dog. The strongest, most durable and most intelligent specimens of Canaan Dog have stood the test of time. They have managed to battle and survive the harsh and demanding conditions of the Israeli environment, while the influx of civiliza-tion has managed to kill off many wild-dog varieties. The Canaan Dog is the official national breed of Israel.

Dr. Rudolphina Menzel, a noted expert in canine studies from Vienna, immigrated to Palestine in 1934. Dr. Menzel was recruited by the "future State of Israel" to develop a service-dog organization for guarding Hebrew settlements and fighting the War of Independence. It wasn't long before Dr. Menzel recognized and turned to the fine qualities of the feral Canaan Dog. Dr. Menzel first earned the respect and trust of the feral Canaani by feeding them near her home, not a new trick in domesticating a dog! She was successful in bringing some puppies into her kennel, where she nurtured and raised them. Surprisingly, Dr. Menzel found the dogs to be very adaptable to domestication. These litters eventually would go on to establish the Canaan Dog breed. Dr. Menzel was the person responsible for naming these feral pariah dogs the "Canaan Dog."

Dr. Menzel is considered by many to be the founder of the breed, the person who deserves credit for the redomestication of the breed. Under her leadership and training, the breed was used as defense forces during and after World War II. In 1948, Dr. Menzel became involved with a guide-dogs-for-the-blind program. In

1949, she founded the Institute for Orientation and Mobility of the Blind, which was the only organization of its kind in the Middle East. By 1948, there were approximately 150 Canaan Dogs registered in its stud book. In 1953, the Israel Kennel Club accepted the breed standard for the Canaan Dog that originally was prepared by Dr. Menzel. Dr. Menzel also was responsible for the first exports to the United States and Europe. She incorporated feral stock into her breeding program from time to time, to keep "original" breed characteristics.

Although the Canaan Dog still exists in fairly large numbers in the wild, their population in the wild is dwindling somewhat because of growing civilization. However, the breed's popularity in the home has grown tremendously in recent years. It has established recognition in countries such as England, Germany, Holland, Switzerland, Finland, France, Austria, Italy, Denmark, South Africa and, of course, the United States. Today, the Canaan Dog can still be found guarding the Bedouin camps and flocks. They are also kept by Arab villagers and farmers to protect livestock.

Israel is responsible for the origin and development of many foundation dogs worldwide. Dr. Menzel's Isr. Ch. Laish me B'nei HaBitachon, "Simi," is one such dog. The very first Israeli champion was Shaar Hagai Kennel's Isr. Ch. Lapid me Shaar Hagai. Sirpad me Shaar Hagai is the breed's top winner and most influential sire. Many believe he was the most perfect example of the breed.

THE CANAAN DOG IN AMERICA

The first Canaan Dogs were exported to the U.S. on September 7, 1965. Mrs. Ursula Berkowitz of Oxnard, California imported the first four Canaan Dogs to establish the breed in the States. These four original dogs were from Dr. Menzel; two of the dogs were from her own breeding and the other two were feral specimens. These four dogs would later go on to be the foundation of the breed in the United States and Canada. Mex. Ch. Toro me Isfija was one of the first dogs sent to America. As many has 75% of registered American dogs today can be traced to Aleph of Star Pine, CCA5.

Mrs. Berkowitz accepted the responsibility of establishing the

DOGS OF WAR

During World War II, Dr. Rudolphina Menzel recruited and trained almost 500 of the best Canaan Dogs for the Middle East armed forces. The dogs were used for tracking, patrolling, sending messages and guarding.

breed in America. Her first litter was whelped in November 1965 by the sire Birion me Bnei HaBitachon and out of the dam HaBitachon Waf me Massada.

It wasn't long before the Canaan Club of America (CCA, now recognized as the Canaan Dog Club of America) was formed, and stud book records were kept from these first imports. Over the years, several more dogs were imported into the States by Dr. Menzel and the Shaar Hagai Kennels. The Shaar Hagai Kennels, located near Jerusalem, were major breeders of Canaan Dogs, using both feral specimens and Dr. Menzel's dogs.

In addition to establishing the breed in the US, Mrs. Berkowitz was instrumental in the development of the Canaan Club of America in 1969. The first president of the club was David Hill. The first American breed

Color patterns in the breed can be with patches of color, as displayed by the male, or a solid color, as seen on the bitch.

TYPE VARIATION IN THE WILD
There are mainly two distinctive types of Canaan Dog in the wild. One variety is referred to as a "collie type" and has an appearance similar to the Border Collie. The other specimen is the "dingo type" and is more primitive and less developed.

standard was adopted in May 1973 and the first official American show took place at Spatterdash Kennels in Emmaus, Pennsylvania on May 28, 1972. There were a total of 14 Canaan Dogs entered at this inaugural event.

It wasn't until June 1, 1989 that the American Kennel Club recognized the Canaan Dog as eligible for the Miscellaneous Class in conformation events. On September 9, 1996, the Board of Directors of the American Kennel Club voted to accept the breed into the AKC registry. Some eight years later, in August 1997, the breed was admitted to the Herding Group and eligible for championships.

In recent decades, there have been many foundation Canaan Dog kennels and dogs in America that have had a major influence on the breed's development. One example was Jay and Bertha Shaeffer's Spatterdash Kennels. The Shaeffers were fundamental in the development of the breed in

How close in origin the Canaan Dog is to the wolf is not known, but the breed's general appearance and expression certainly resemble those of their lupine ancestors.

the United States. Two of their top dogs that earned great recognition were Spatterdash Yawvin and Mex. Ch. Hora me Shaar Hagai.

The long list of instrumental American breeders, kennels and dogs is quite substantial; following is just a partial list: William and Lorraine Stephens (Geva Canaan Dogs); Bryna Comsky (Ha'Aretz Canaan Dogs); Donna Dodson (Pleasant Hill); Hinda Bergman (Beth Din Canaani) and Ellen Klein (Briel Kennels).

Bryna Comsky was the first Canaan owner to earn a Tracking Dog title. Donna Dodson had multiple specialty winners, and Hinda Bergman was responsible for Int. Mex. World CCA and Ch. Beth Din Witch's Brew. These dogs established themselves as top winners in the ring and great examples of the breed.

Some other top-winning dogs included CCA Ch. Lahatut me Shaar Hagai, UD (first Utility Dog, a top title in American obedience trials), and Padre's Shekvar von Karstadt, who was one of the first to earn a Best in Show.

THE CANAAN DOG IN THE UNITED KINGDOM

Because of the strong efforts of Mrs. Connie Higgins, the Canaan Dog was recognized in England on December 31, 1970. Mrs. Higgins' involvement with the breed began when she adopted a bitch

('Shebaba') that was wild-born in Syria and brought to England by another owner. Like many other Canaan enthusiasts, Mrs. Higgins had correspondence with Dr. Rudolphina Menzel. She asked Dr. Menzel to rate the dog and inquired whether she felt that her bitch should be bred. Dr. Menzel approved of the bitch and shipped a black and white male named Tiron to accomplish the breeding. The Kennel Club accepted Tiron and Shebaba. Shebaba would become the last dog of unknown heritage to be registered by The Kennel Club. This was the beginning of the Canaan Dog in England and, in 1970, The Kennel Club officially recognized the breed.

The objective of the breed's parent club was to promote the interests of the Canaan Dog in Great Britain and safeguard the

BRAIN AND BRAWN

Since dogs have been bred for centuries, their physical and mental characteristics are constantly being changed to suit man's desires for hunting, retrieving, scenting, guarding and warming their masters' laps. During the past 150 years, dogs have been judged according to physical characteristics as well as functional abilities. Few breeds can boast a genuine balance between physique, working ability and temperament.

characteristics of this unique breed. There was a group of seven individuals on the club's steering committee. The committee included Mary MacPhail, Ron Graham, Steve Payne, Jan Smith, Helen Lightfoot, Gina Pointing (secretary) and Phil Smith (treasurer). The first meeting of this steering committee, which formed the Canaan Dog Club (CDC), took place at the Pine Lodge Hotel near Bromsgrove.

At first, breed interest was very limited. It wasn't until 1981 that the next wave of interest in the breed rose. Ruth Tribe Corner reintroduced the breed to England after returning from Israel. In the late 1970s, she joined Myrna Shiboleth and Dvora Ben Shaul in Israel. She worked at and helped run the kennels for four years. Mrs. Corner was fascinated with the Canaan breed and thoroughly enjoyed training and caring for the dogs. Mrs. Corner left Israel at the end of 1981 and returned to the United Kingdom. At that time, there were no known Canaani in Britain.

In 1986, Mrs. Corner imported two pregnant Canaan bitches from Israel. Once the puppies were born and weaned, the bitches returned to Israel. The litters would go on to produce several top specimens. Mrs. Corner was able to show the dogs quite successfully in England, Wales and Scotland for two years at most major Championship Shows, including the prestigious Crufts. David and Marjorie Cording, Mary MacPhail and Gina Pointing also purchased dogs from these original litters and were extremely helpful in showing and promoting the breed in England during the late 1980s. The Cordings and Mary McPhail would later co-own Kensix Khaneshee, who would go on to become a top-winning dog

Recognized in the UK in 1970, the Canaan Dog has had its ups and downs there, but now is a growing breed. Pictured here is a Canaan Dog competing in a UK conformation show.

in the country. The increase in the breed's popularity helped the formation of the Canaan Club of England in May 1992.

Unfortunately, in 1994, Mrs. Corner encountered difficulties that led to her losing her home and business, and she had to give up her dogs. However, her tremendous influence in the breed's development cannot be denied. Her articles and breed notes helped greatly with the promotion of the breed in the UK.

Today, the Canaan Dog continues to grow strong in the United Kingdom. In recent years, thanks to the efforts of Richard Minto and Ellen Klein, the Canaan Dogs of Anacan emerged. Mr. Minto and Ms. Klein teamed up as chairman and club secretary of the CDC, and their efforts have assisted the growth of the breed. In recent years, thanks to the dedication and enthusiastic interest of many new faces, the Canaan is finally gaining the respect and credibility it rightfully deserves. All indications point to the Canaan Dog's continuing to grow in strength in the United Kingdom.

The Canaan Dog attracts fanciers who are fascinated by the breed's unique background, complex personality and natural beauty.

The Canaan Dog is an unspoiled breed, not modified in any way for exhibition purposes. Breeders who concentrate their efforts on preserving the breed's true characteristics wouldn't have it any other way!

CHARACTERISTICS OF THE
CANAAN DOG

IS THE CANAAN DOG RIGHT FOR YOU?

Before you decide to purchase or bring home any type of dog, you must be sure that you've chosen one that will be compatible with your home environment. We each have our own distinct lifestyles, and therefore the requirements of certain breeds do not always fit our own needs and expectations. To make sure that the breed you choose is what you think it is, it's smart to do your homework. Visit the local library or bookstore, or search in internet, and read all of the information available on your breed of choice, the Canaan Dog. Go to an all-breed dog show or a Canaan Dog specialty show. Contact reliable Canaan Dog owners and breeders. Make arrangements to visit reputable Canaan kennels and meet the dogs.

Spend as much time as you can around the breed. Carefully observe the breed's behavior and characteristics. Once you've finished your in-depth research, you must still ask yourself whether the requirements of the Canaan Dog match your lifestyle. If they don't, you must be honest with yourself and choose a dog that more closely matches your expectations.

The Canaan Dog is a valued companion dog and working dog. The breed possesses extremely keen senses of hearing and smell and can detect approaching intruders from a considerable distance. Canaan Dogs are extremely loyal to their families, but can be aloof when confronted with strange people and other unfamiliar things. Canaan Dogs, by nature, are a bit standoffish. They sometimes don't socialize well with other dogs and may even have some difficulty adjusting to other pets in the home. These distinct characteristics may not make them "ideal" pets, and careful consideration must be given before introducing a Canaan

"THOSE CANAAN DAYS"

Today, the Canaan Dog is still used to guard the Bedouin camps and flocks. The people of Israel have come to value the unique qualities of their native breed and frequently use the dogs as protectors of their homes.

Although Canaani typically thrive best in one-dog homes, they certainly can be socialized. Friendship between canine housemates depends much upon the care and effort that the human family puts into developing it.

Dog to a home environment that already has dogs or other animals present.

Canaan Dogs are usually at their best when there are no other animals in the home, but this is not to say that they won't socialize with dogs, cats and possibly other pets. How the Canaan Dog behaves with other animals depends on whether all parties concerned have been properly acquainted with one another. Given the breed's prey instincts, Canaan Dogs should not be trusted with small-mammal pets like guinea pigs or rabbits. They can get along fine with cats, but extra precautions, supervision and patience are recommended. Canaan Dogs, typical of herding-type dogs, tend not to get along too well with other dogs, especially members of the same sex. The best way to deal with this type of dog-aggression is to socialize the Canaan Dog from puppyhood into adulthood with other dogs.

The breed has a strong desire to guard and is very territorial, making them excellent watchdogs.

THE CANAAN HOUDINI
Canaan Dogs are extremely intelligent and creative. They are expert escape artists. It is not uncommon for them to escape from a fenced-in yard or pen. For the breed's safety, it's important to take extra precautions when attempting to keep your Canaan confined.

Since the breed has not been domesticated for all that long, many of its feral-dog qualities are certain to come to the fore in different situations. The Canaan Dog behaves like no other dog and may not be for everyone. Although all dogs are possessive and territorial, the Canaan holds more of these qualities than most any other breed. Canaan Dogs will bark wildly and circle when intruders approach. They are frequently very insecure when taken out of their home environments. Unlike some other breeds, bitches are just as territorial as males and will mark their territory just as much as the

HAVE YOU HERD?
Although not specifically bred for herding like the Border Collie or Australian Cattle Dog, the Canaan Dog does maintain a strong desire to herd, a trait used by individuals for thousands of years. The breed has been used successfully on farms to herd ducks, sheep, goats, horses and cattle. In America, the Canaan Dog is routinely tested in sanctioned herding events. The breed's high degree of intelligence and ability to learn commands quickly make them assured stockdogs. The Canaan Dog also has a strong natural drive ability, which requires minimal training to develop.

males will. Keen of hearing, the Canaan is capable of alerting his owners to someone's approaching long before other dogs seem to be aware of a possible intrusion.

Socialization is very important with this breed. The breed must learn to deal with strange people and surroundings. This is not always as easy as it may seem. The breed has a natural instinct to guard and to be cautious, which must be modified for the sake of good canine behavior. You must remember that, in the wild, Canaan Dogs had to be naturally aggressive to survive. In the wild, they needed to fight over territory, food, etc., and were sometimes forced to fight until death. In the wild, there is a distinctive "pecking order" and it's not unusual for Canaani to test or challenge the chain of command in the home environment.

Socialization is the key to building trust and a bond between the Canaan and all members of the family. Canaani and children get along best when both canine and human "kids" grow up together.

CANAAN TYPE DIFFERENCES

There are two main types of Canaan Dog in the United States and England. There is the original Border Collie/Kelpie stockdog-type dog that was sent to the United States and England by Dr. Rudolphina Menzel. The second type is the heavier, thick-coated variety of Myrna Shiboleth of Shaar Hagai Kennels in Israel. In addition to differences in type, breeders report variation in temperament and herding ability between the two.

The Canaan Dog must be taught at an early age to trust and depend on his owner; this will certainly help to build the dog's confidence as he matures. It's important to socialize Canaani with other dogs, children and adults. The more socialization, the better the dog will get along with other dogs and people outside the family.

The Canaan Dog is extremely loyal and devoted, but can be aggressive toward unfamiliar humans. They won't think twice about biting to defend their territory and cherished family members. However, they are not "one-man dogs" and are usually devoted to the entire family. They are very good with children, of whom they are usually very protective. When brought up with young people, the Canaan will bond with them almost immediately and quickly become a devoted family companion and natural watchdog. Because of the breed's strong denning instinct, due to their wild-dog heritage, they are naturally clean, like cats, and easily house-trained.

Despite their sometimes reserved temperaments, the Canaan Dog is a highly intelligent and trainable breed that possesses excellent tracking ability. Likewise, the Canaan is a tremendous herding dog and performs very well in sanctioned stockdog events. The Canaan Dog also has been trained successfully for many different types of tracking tasks. Without a doubt, the Canaan Dog is capable of many varied tasks. Canaan Dogs develop very close working relationships with their owners and will usually obey out of respect for their pack leaders. It's important for the Canaan owner to find out what motivates his dog and to develop a "working team" attitude while training.

In ancient times, the dogs were able to thrive in difficult desert conditions and terrain. Today, the breed still has an immense adaptability to climate changes, being able to adjust to both cold and warm climates. They make excellent urban dogs, as well as great farm dogs and rural pets.

The Canaan Dog's high level of intelligence can lead to some dogs' being severely stubborn. They are quick learners, but big thinkers. If they feel that they are right and you are wrong, they won't hesitate to do things their own way. This can make training this headstrong breed difficult at times. However, once Canaani understand who the boss is, they will respond quickly to training and go to great extremes to please their owners. They usually pick up basic commands rather easily.

Like other intelligent herding breeds, Canaan Dogs can get bored easily. They need training programs that are both creative and stimulating. The breed enjoys variety and disapproves of routine. If housed in a kennel or on a large piece of property, it's not uncommon for a Canaan Dog to dig holes or build a cave-like retreat. Canaani also enjoy burying things.

HUNTING BY SIGHT
The Canaan Dog has tremendous eyesight. In fact, its vision is almost as good as that of some sighthounds. In the wild, they use their tremendous sight and incredibly keen sense of smell to hunt down small game for food.

The Canaan Dog, like all other breeds, requires positive reinforcement in training. If you train using harsh methods, the Canaan will quickly learn that training is not fun and he will not respond. Canaan Dogs have long memories and will remember harsh punishment more than any reward. They will respect their owners, but only if the owners earn it and show them respect in return. Training sessions should always be positive, with lots of praise and rewards. You must always remember that the Canaan is very pack-oriented, and even the most passive dog will take over in a house where no pack leader has established himself.

Believe it or not, despite the breed's tremendous athletic ability, Canaani do not need excessive amounts of exercise. A brisk 20–30-minute walk daily will keep a Canaan Dog in ideal physical shape; two shorter walks will also suffice nicely. Canaani do enjoy the freedom and independence of roaming in large enclosed spaces. Allowing the Canaan to have a high-speed romp around your fenced property will likely tire him out for the day.

Unless your dog has had extensive obedience training, you may want to think twice before taking him off-lead in public places. Some have been known to be unreliable off-lead; plus, you should always consider leash laws in your community. Most spitz and

DOGS, DOGS, GOOD FOR YOUR HEART!

People usually purchase dogs for companionship, but studies show that dogs can help to improve their owners' health and level of activity, as well as lower a human's risk of coronary heart disease. Without even realizing it, when a person puts time into exercising, grooming and feeding a dog, he also puts more time into his own personal health care. Dog owners establish programs for their dogs to follow, which can have positive effects on their health. Dogs also teach us patience, offer unconditional love and provide the joy of having a furry friend to pet!

pariah-type dogs will run when given the opportunity. Taking a Canaan off his lead is an open invitation to go explore the world—if afforded the chance, your Canaan Dog will be feral in about 24 hours!

BREED STANDARD FOR THE
CANAAN DOG

All of the breeds currently recognized by the American Kennel Club, The Kennel Club in Britain or the Fédération Cynologique Internationale have an official breed standard, which varies from country to country but is essentially quite similar. The standard characterizes the description of the ideal representative of a breed, both physically and temperamentally. The standard is not the description of any actual dog, but simply a theory set forth by breed experts. A breed standard is used as a measuring stick by which to judge a breed at dog shows.

In a typical conformation show, a judge will evaluate every competitor that is shown under him. The dog that most closely resembles the standard, by the judge's determination, is the dog that should be placed first in its class. Not every judge agrees on which dog or dogs are best. That's what makes conformation competition exciting and appealing to the show-dog hobbyist. Each show features a different judging panel with different opinions as to which competitors most closely adhere to the standard.

The breed standard is a very valuable asset for both the novice and experienced Canaan Dog owner, breeder and show judge. Any person interested in buying a puppy or adult dog should thoroughly study the breed standard. It is a valuable guide to recognizing the essential qualities that make up your breed of choice. It's very helpful to familiarize yourself with the breed's major faults and/or disqualifications. This will help when it comes time to purchase a dog and help you to avoid potential problems. Although the "perfect" dog portrayed in the breed standard will never exist, it is in your (and the breed's) best interest to attempt to obtain a dog that closely resembles the standard.

THE AMERICAN KENNEL CLUB STANDARD FOR THE CANAAN DOG

GENERAL APPEARANCE
The Canaan Dog is a herding and flock guardian dog native to the Middle East. He is aloof with strangers, inquisitive, loyal and loving with his family. His

This Best of Breed winner was the highlight of the Canaan Dog breed at a recent Crufts Dog Show, the largest and most prestigious show in the UK.

medium-size, square body is without extremes, showing a clear, sharp outline. The Canaan Dog moves with athletic agility and grace in a quick, brisk, ground-covering trot. He has a wedge-shaped head with low-set erect ears, a bushy tail that curls over the back when excited, and a straight, harsh, flat-lying double coat.

SIZE, PROPORTION, SUBSTANCE

Size—Height at the withers is 20 to 24 inches for dogs and 19 to 23 inches for bitches. The ideal Canaan Dog lies in the middle of the stated ranges. *Disqualifications*—Dogs less than 20 inches or more than 25 inches. Bitches less than 18 inches or more than 23 inches. *Proportion*—Square when measured from the point of the withers to the base of the tail and from the point of the withers to the ground. *Substance*—Moderate. Dogs generally weigh 45 to 55 pounds and bitches approximately 35 to 45 pounds. Dogs distinctly masculine without coarseness and bitches feminine without over-refinement.

Typical Canaan male, exhibiting coat in full prime and correct type, balance and substance.

HEAD

Elongated, the length exceeding the breadth and depth considerably. Wedge-shaped, when viewed from above. Slightly arched when viewed from the side, tapering to stop. The region of the forehead is of medium width, but appearing broader through ears set low to complete an alert expression, with a slight furrow between the eyes. *Expression*—Alert, watchful, and inquisitive. Dignified. *Eyes*—Dark, almond shaped, slightly slanted. Varying shades of hazel with liver pointed dogs. Eye rims darkly pigmented or of varying shades of liver, harmonizing with coat color. *Fault*—Unpigmented eye rims. *Ears*—Erect, medium to large, set moderately low, broad at the base, tapering to a very slightly rounded tip. Ears angled very slightly forward when excited. A straight line from the inner corner of the ear to the tip of the nose should just touch the inner corner of the eye and a line drawn from the tip of the ear to the tip of the nose should just touch the outer corner of the eye. Ear motion contributes to expression and clearly defines the mood of the dog. *Major Fault*—In the adult dog, other than erect ears. *Stop*—Slightly accentuated. *Muzzle*—Tapering to complete the wedge shape of the head. Length equal to or slightly longer than the length of the skull from the occiput to stop. Whisker trimming optional. *Nose*—Darkly pigmented

Head study, showing correct type and proportion as well as correct ear size and ear set.

or of varying shades of liver, harmonizing with coat color. *Lips*—Tight with good pigmentation. *Bite*—Scissors.

NECK, TOPLINE, BODY

Neck—Well arched. Balance to body and head and free from throatiness. *Topline*—Level with slight arch over the loins. *Body*—Strong, displaying athletic agility and trimness. *Chest*—Moderately broad and deep, extending to the elbows, with well-sprung ribs. *Loin*—Well tucked up. Short, muscled flanks. *Tail*—Set moderately high. May be carried curled over the back when excited; limited to one full curl. When extended, the bone must reach to

There is significant difference between the sexes. The male (left) usually carries a heavier coat and generally has more substance than the bitch (right).

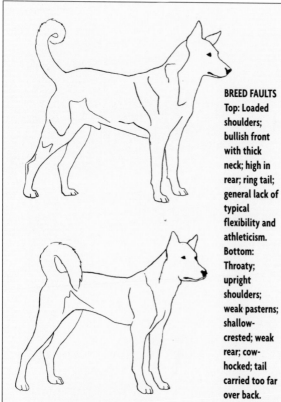

BREED FAULTS Top: Loaded shoulders; bullish front with thick neck; high in rear; ring tail; general lack of typical flexibility and athleticism. Bottom: Throaty; upright shoulders; weak pasterns; shallow-crested; weak rear; cow-hocked; tail carried too far over back.

the hocks. *Fault*—Tail which falls over to either side of the back.

FOREQUARTERS
Shoulders moderately angulated. Legs straight. Pasterns flexible with very slight slope when viewed from the side. Dewclaws may be removed. *Feet*—Catlike, pads hard, pigmentation harmonizing with nose and eye rims. Nails strong, hard, pigmentation harmonizing with either nose and eye rims or coat.

HINDQUARTERS
Moderately angulated. In balance with forequarters. Straight when viewed from the rear. Thigh musculature well developed, moderately broad. Hocks well let down. Dewclaws must be removed. Feet and nails as in forequarters.

COAT

Double coat. Outer coat—straight, harsh, flat-lying, with slight ruff. Ruff more pronounced on males. Length of other coat 1/2 to 1 1/2 inches; longer on ruff and back of thighs, shorter on body, legs, and head. Undercoat—straight, soft, short, flat-lying, density varying with climate. Tail bushy, increasing in plumage from set to end of bones, then tapering to pointed tip. *Faults*—Excessively long guard coat that masks the clean outline of the dog. Any trimming that alters the natural appearance of the dog.

COLOR

There are two color patterns. Pattern 1) Predominately white with mask and with or without additional patches of color (large body patches are desirable). Pattern 2) Solid colored with or without white trim. Color may range from black through all shades of brown—sandy to red or liver. Shadings of black on a solid brown or tan dog are frequently seen. The trim on a solid colored dog may include chest, undercarriage, feet and lower part of leg and tip of tail. In all color patterns self-ticking may be present. *Disqualifications*—a) Gray and/or brindle. b) All white.

MASK

The mask is a desired and distinguishing feature of the predomi-nately white Canaan Dog. The mask is the same color(s) as the body patches on the dog. The basically symmetrical mask must completely cover the eyes and ears or can completely cover the head as in a hood. The only allowed white in the mask or hood is a white blaze of any size or shape and/or white on the muzzle below the mask. *Faults*—On predomi-nately white dogs—absence of

BREED FAULTS
Top: Upright, loaded shoulders; dip in topline behind shoulders; arch over loin with low tail set; weak rear.
Bottom: Ewe-necked; upright shoulders; lack of proper angulation in rear.

mask, half mask or grossly asymmetrical mask.

Gait

Movement is very important. Good reach and drive. Quick, brisk natural trot, apparently tireless, indicating an animal capable of trotting for hours. Covers ground more quickly than expected. Agile, able to change directions almost instantaneously. Tends to single track at high speed. *Fault*—Anything that detracts from efficient movement.

Temperament

Alert, vigilant, devoted and docile with his family. Reserved and aloof with strangers. Highly territorial, serving as a responsive companion and natural guardian. Very vocal, persistent. Easily trained. *Faults*—Shyness or dominance towards people.

The Canaan Dog's gait is very important, as the dog must be an agile athlete, quick on his feet, with a brisk natural trot that is tireless. The gait is evaluated in the show ring to ensure that typical movement has not been lost in show dogs.

SELECTING A CANAAN DOG

A REPUTABLE BREEDER

Your Canaan Dog should only be purchased from a breeder who has earned a reputation for consistently producing dogs that are mentally and physically sound. The only way a breeder can earn this reputation is through selective breeding aimed at eliminating genetic weaknesses.

The first question a prospective owner should ask a Canaan Dog breeder is, "What do you do with your dogs?" If the person you are talking to breeds Canaan Dogs only to sell—go somewhere else for your dog! Dedicated Canaan Dog breeders belong to their breed club, compete at shows and are adamant about proper socialization of their dogs.

These same people are very much aware of who else in the breed does or does not ascribe to the breed club's rigid Code of Ethics. It is a requirement of the club that all dogs are hip scored to ascertain the degree, if any, of hip problems. Responsible breeders are the individuals upon whom you can depend in your quest to obtain a sound, well-bred and well-socialized representative of the Canaan Dog breed.

The first clue that tells you how much the breeder cares about his dogs is the cleanliness of the area in which the dogs are kept. The next is how well socialized the parents of the litter are. Those two conditions met, you can proceed to look at the puppies themselves.

The breeder may ask you so many questions that you may feel like you are on trial. In a way, you are...everyone is not the ideal owner of a Canaan! The breeder is considering whether or not you would make a good owner of a Canaan Dog and, if so, which puppy in the litter would be most suitable for you.

PUPPY VERSUS ADULT

Since you've selected the Canaan Dog as your breed of choice, you must determine whether you have your heart set on a puppy or whether an adult dog would be a better choice. Your decision might be entirely based on what type of dogs are available in your area. The Canaan puppy holds some distinct advantages over the adult dog. The puppy can be taught to socialize with other dogs, pets and children. Attempting to socialize an older dog that is not used to these might be difficult.

PICKING YOUR PUP

Once you've located a reliable breeder, make arrangements to see the puppies they have for sale. If you cannot locate puppies in your area, you may want to contact your national kennel club (e.g., the American Kennel Club, Kennel Club in Britain, etc.) or the breed's parent club for a list of Canaan breeders.

When visiting the breeder, be sure to ask as many questions as you deem necessary. Examine the health and temperaments of the pups and the adult dogs on the premises. Do they appear to be socializing well with each other? Are they friendly, or do they appear hostile or timid? Odds are, if the puppies are not showing pleasant personalities at the puppy stage, they won't as adults either.

The average litter size is four puppies, so selection will be somewhat limited once you've located a litter. The price of puppies varies from breeder to breeder and dog to dog. Because litters are small and because the Canaan Dog is a relatively rare breed, commercial breeders thankfully are not attracted to the breed. This also helps your

selection, ensuring that most pups will come from strong working lines unencumbered by overbreeding, inbreeding or unfortunate prejudices that have damaged other, more popular, breeds. The amount you spend on a dog depends on whether you are interested in a pet, a show dog or a dog that can compete in agility, tracking, obedience, herding and other activities.

Since you are likely choosing a Canaan Dog as a pet dog and not a working dog, you simply should select a pup that is friendly and attractive. Since there are two different types of Canaani, the stockdog type and the heavier-coated thicker type, you must be aware of the variation in temperament and trainability. In any case, beware of the shy or overly aggressive puppy, and be especially conscious of the nervous Canaan Dog pup. Likewise, don't let sentiment or emotion trap you into buying a puppy that is sickly, bloated, too thin or otherwise less than healthy-looking.

Healthy Canaan Dog puppies are strong and firm to the touch,

A HEALTHY PUP
You should not even think about buying a puppy that looks sick, undernourished, overly frightened or nervous. Sometimes a timid puppy will warm up to you after a 30-minute "let's-get-acquainted" session.

never bony or, on the other hand, obese and bloated. Coats will be shiny with no sign of dry or flaky skin, though stockdog types will have thinner coats than the heavier-coated dogs. The inside of the puppy's ears should be pink and clean. Dark discharge or a bad odor could indicate ear mites, a sure sign of poor maintenance. The healthy Canaan puppy's breath smells sweet. The teeth are clean and white, and there should never be any malformation of the mouth or jaw. The puppy's eyes should be clear and bright. Eyes that appear runny and irritated could indicate serious problems. There should be no sign of discharge from the nose, nor should it ever be crusted or runny. Coughing and diarrhea are danger signals, as are any eruptions on the skin.

If you have intentions of using your new charge for herding, there are more considerations. The parents of a future working dog should have excellent qualifications, including actual work experience as well as working titles in their pedigrees. Perhaps the sire or dam has competed and titled in herding trials. A Versatility Award is also a plus for a Canaan Dog.

The gender of your puppy is largely a matter of personal taste, although there is a common belief among those who work with herding dogs that bitches are quicker to learn and generally

YOUR SCHEDULE ...

If you lead an erratic, unpredictable life, with daily or weekly changes in your work requirements, consider the problems of owning a puppy. The new puppy has to be fed regularly, socialized (loved, petted, handled, introduced to other people) and, most importantly, allowed to go outdoors for house-training. As the dog gets older, it can be more tolerant of deviations in its feeding and relief schedule.

more loving and faithful. Males are more aggressive and learn more slowly. The difference in size is noticeable, though not significant.

PREPARING PUPPY'S PLACE IN YOUR HOME

Researching your breed and finding a breeder are only two aspects of the homework you will have to do before collecting your

ARE YOU PREPARED?

Unfortunately, when a puppy is bought by someone who does not take into consideration the time and attention that dog ownership requires, it is the puppy who suffers when he is either abandoned or placed in a shelter by a frustrated owner. So all of the homework you do in preparation for your pup's arrival will benefit you both. The more informed you are, the more you will know what to expect and the better equipped you will be to handle the ups and downs of raising a puppy. Hopefully, everyone in the household is willing to do his part in raising and caring for the pup. The anticipation of owning a dog often brings a lot of promises from excited family members: "I will walk him every day," "I will feed him," "I will house-train him," etc., but these things take time and effort, and promises can easily be forgotten once the novelty of the new pet has worn off.

Canaan puppy. You will also have to prepare your home and family for the new addition. Much as you would prepare a nursery for a newborn baby, you will need to designate a place in your home that will be the puppy's own. How you prepare your home will depend on how much freedom the dog will be allowed. Whatever you decide, you must ensure that he has a place that he can "call his own."

When you bring your new puppy into your home, you are bringing him into what will become his home as well. Obviously, you did not buy a puppy with the intention of catering to his every whim and allowing him to "rule the roost," but in order for a puppy to grow into a stable, well-adjusted dog, he has to feel comfortable in his surroundings. Remember, he is

What's a more charming sight than a pile of snoozing Canaan pups?

TEMPERAMENT COUNTS

Your selection of a good puppy can be determined by your needs. A show potential or a good pet? It is your choice. Every puppy, however, should be of good temperament. Although show-quality puppies are bred and raised with emphasis on physical conformation, responsible breeders strive for equally good temperament. Do not buy from a breeder who concentrates solely on physical beauty at the expense of personality.

leaving the warmth and security of his mother and littermates, as well as the familiarity of the only place he has ever known, so it is important to make his transition as easy as possible. By preparing a place in your home for the puppy, you are making him feel as welcome as possible in a strange new place. It should not take him long to get used to it, but the sudden shock of being transplanted is somewhat traumatic for a young pup. Imagine how a small child would feel in the same situation—that is how your puppy must be feeling. It is up to you to reassure him and to let him know, "Little fellow, you are going to like it here!"

WHAT YOU SHOULD BUY

CRATE

To someone unfamiliar with the use of crates in dog training, it may seem like punishment to shut a dog in a crate, but this is not the case at all. Crate training is recommended by breeders for show and pet puppies alike. Do not equate the crate with a prison cell or solitary confinement—you must think like a dog. A crate is the dog's den and is the most useful tool we have in house-training a puppy and teaching the dog structure, a virtue not readily accepted by Canaani. In addition, a crate can keep your dog safe during travel and, perhaps most

PUPPY APPEARANCE

Your puppy should have a well-fed appearance but not a distended abdomen, which may indicate worms or incorrect feeding, or both. The body should be firm, with a solid feel. The skin of the abdomen should be pale pink and clean, without signs of scratching or rash. Check the hind legs to make certain that the dewclaws have been removed.

Your local pet shop will have a variety of crates. Choose a durable crate for your Canaan puppy that is large enough to accommodate him when full grown.

PHOTO COURTESY OF DOSKOCIL.

just happen to be providing him with something a little more luxurious than what his wild relations enjoyed.

As far as purchasing a crate, the type that you buy is up to you. It will most likely be one of the two most popular types: wire or fiberglass. There are advantages and disadvantages to each type. For example, a wire crate is more open, allowing the air to flow through and affording the dog a view of what is going on around him, while a fiberglass crate is sturdier. Both can double

importantly, a crate provides your dog with a place of his own in your home. It serves as a "doggie bedroom" of sorts—your Canaan puppy can curl up in his crate when he wants to sleep or when he just needs a break. Many dogs sleep in their crates overnight. With soft bedding and his favorite toy, a crate becomes a cozy pseudo-den for your dog. Like his ancestors, he too will seek out the comfort and retreat of a den—you

CRATE-TRAINING TIPS

During crate training, you should partition off the section of the crate in which the pup stays. If he is given too big an area, this will hinder your training efforts. Crate training is based on the fact that a dog does not like to soil his sleeping quarters, so it is ineffective to keep a pup in an area that is so big that he can eliminate in one end and get far enough away from it to sleep. Also, you want to make the crate den-like for the pup. Blankets and a favorite toy will make the crate cozy for the small pup; as he grows, you may want to evict some of his "roommates" to make more room. It will take some coaxing at first, but be patient. Given some time to get used to it, your pup will adapt to his new home-within-a-home quite nicely.

Snuggling with his littermates is comforting to a pup, so you must create a cozy, welcoming place in your home for the pup to call his own.

"YOU BETTER SHOP AROUND!"

Finding a reputable breeder who sells healthy pups is very important, but make sure that the breeder you choose is not only someone you respect but also someone with whom you feel comfortable. Your breeder will be a resource long after you buy your puppy, and you must be able to call with reasonable questions without being made to feel like a pest! If you don't connect on a personal level, investigate some other breeders before making a final decision.

as travel crates, providing protection for the dog. A medium- to large-size crate will be necessary for a full-grown Canaan Dog.

BEDDING

Soft bedding in the dog's crate will help the dog feel more at home, and you may also like to provide a small blanket. First, this will take the place of the leaves, twigs, etc., that the pup would use in the wild to make a den; the pup can make his own "burrow" in the crate. The Canaan Dog's denning instinct is still a vibrant part of his genetic make-up, and he will be thankful for your thoughtful accommodation. Second, until you take your pup home, he has been sleeping amid the warmth of his mother and littermates, and while a blanket is not the same as a warm, breathing body, it still provides heat and something with which to snuggle. You will want to wash your pup's bedding frequently in case he has a house-training mishap in his crate, and replace or remove any blanket that becomes ragged and starts to fall apart.

TOYS

Toys are a must for dogs of all ages, especially for curious playful pups. Puppies are the "children" of the dog world, and what child does not love toys? Chew toys provide enjoyment for both dog and owner—your dog will enjoy playing with his favorite toys, while you will enjoy the fact that they distract him from chewing on your expensive shoes and leather sofa. Puppies love to chew; in fact, chewing is a physical need for pups as they are teething, and everything looks appetizing! The full range of your possessions—from cotton slipper to Oriental carpet—are fair game in the eyes of a teething pup. Puppies are not all that discerning when it comes to finding something literally to "sink their teeth into"—everything tastes great!

Though not inveterate chewers, a bored Canaan Dog with nothing to do and insufficient human contact can become a destructive Canaan Dog. Chewing is one way the breed can release some of the frustration that builds up. To prevent destructive chewing from occurring, select durable toys for both puppies and adults that are designed for powerfully jawed dogs and make sure your dog is receiving the attention and activity that he deserves.

TEETHING TIP

Puppies like soft toys for chewing. Because they are teething, soft items like stuffed toys soothe their aching gums. Offer soft toys under close supervision.

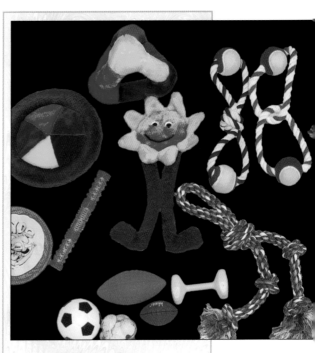

TOYS, TOYS, TOYS!

With a big variety of dog toys available, and so many that look like they would be a lot of fun for a dog, be careful in your selection. It is amazing what a set of puppy teeth can do to an innocent-looking toy; so, obviously, safety is a major consideration. Be sure to choose the most durable products that you can find. Hard nylon bones and toys are a safe bet, and many of them are offered in different scents and flavors that will be sure to capture your dog's attention. It is always fun to play a game of fetch with your dog, and there are balls and flying discs that are specially made to withstand dog teeth.

MENTAL AND DENTAL

Toys help your puppy get the physical and mental stimulation he needs. Hard rubber or nylon toys are designed to scrape away plaque, preventing bad breath and gum infection. Soft toys are welcomed by teething pups but should be monitored as these toys can be easily destroyed.

From the wide array of leads available, you will be able to find one suitable for your Canaan Dog.

Squeaky toys are quite popular, but must be avoided for the Canaan Dog. Perhaps a squeaky toy can be used as an aid in training, but not for free play. If a pup "disembowels" one of these, the small plastic squeaker inside can be dangerous if swallowed. Monitor the condition of all your pup's toys carefully and get rid of any that have been chewed to the point of becoming potentially dangerous.

Be careful of natural bones, which have a tendency to splinter into sharp, dangerous pieces. Also be careful of rawhide, which can turn into pieces that are easy to swallow and become a mushy mess on your carpet.

LEAD

A nylon lead is probably the best option, as it is the most resistant to puppy teeth should your pup take a liking to chewing on his lead. Of course, this is a habit that should be nipped in the bud, but, if your pup likes to chew on his lead, he has a very slim chance of being able to chew through the strong nylon. Nylon leads are also lightweight, which is good for a young Canaan Dog who is just getting used to the idea of walking on a lead. For everyday walking and safety purposes, the nylon lead is a good choice.

As your pup grows up and gets used to walking on the lead,

FINANCIAL RESPONSIBILITY

Grooming tools, collars, leashes, a crate, a dog bed and, of course, toys will be expenses to you when you first obtain your pup, and the cost will continue throughout your dog's lifetime. If your puppy damages or destroys your possessions (as most puppies surely will!) or something belonging to a neighbor, you can calculate additional expense. There is also flea and pest control, which every dog owner faces more than once. You must be able to handle the financial responsibility of owning a dog.

you may want to purchase a flexible lead. These leads allow you to extend the length to give the dog a broader area to explore or to shorten the length to keep the dog near you. Of course, there are leads designed for training purposes and specially made leather harnesses, but these are not necessary for routine walks.

COLLAR

Your pup should get used to wearing a collar all the time since you will want to attach his identification tags to it; plus, you have to attach the lead to something! A lightweight nylon collar is a good choice. Make certain that the collar fits snugly enough so that the pup cannot wriggle out of it, but is loose enough so that it will not be uncomfortably tight around the pup's neck. You should be able to fit a finger between the pup's neck and the collar. It may take some time for your pup to get used to wearing the collar, but soon he will not even notice that it is there. Choke collars are made for training, but

should only be used by those who know exactly how to use them.

FOOD AND WATER BOWLS

Your pup will need two bowls, one for food and one for water. You may want two sets of bowls, one for indoors and one for outdoors, depending on where the dog will be fed and where he

The collar needed for an adult Canaan will be thicker and stronger than that needed for a pup. This dog has a sturdy nylon lead and collar with his ID tags attached.

CHOOSE AN APPROPRIATE COLLAR

The **BUCKLE COLLAR** is the standard collar used for everyday purposes. Be sure that you adjust the buckle on growing puppies. Check it every day. It can become too tight overnight! These collars can be made of leather or nylon. Attach your dog's identification tags to this collar.

The **CHOKE COLLAR** is constructed of highly polished steel so that it slides easily through the stainless steel loop. The idea is that the dog controls the pressure around his neck and he will stop pulling if the collar becomes uncomfortable. It is used *only* for training and should *never* be left on a dog.

The **HALTER** is for a trained dog that has to be restrained to prevent running away, chasing a cat and the like. Considered the most humane of all collars, it is frequently used on smaller dogs on which collars are not comfortable.

will be spending time. Purchase the largest size you can find. Stainless steel or sturdy plastic bowls are popular choices. Plastic bowls are more chewable, but dogs tend not to chew on the steel variety, which can be sterilized. It is important to buy sturdy bowls since anything is in danger of being chewed by puppy teeth and you do not want your dog to be constantly chewing apart his bowl (for his safety and for your financial stability!).

CLEANING SUPPLIES
Until a pup is house-trained, you will be doing a lot of cleaning. "Accidents" will occur, which is acceptable in the beginning stages of house-training because the puppy does not know any better. All you can do is be prepared to clean up any accidents as soon as they happen. Old rags, towels, newspapers and a safe disinfectant are good to have on hand.

BEYOND THE BASICS
The items previously discussed are the bare necessities. You will find out what else you need as you go along—grooming supplies, flea/tick protection, baby gates to partition a room, etc. These things will vary depending on your situation, but it is important that you have everything you need to feed and make your Canaan Dog comfortable in his first few days at home.

Your local pet shop will have an array of dishes and bowls suitable for the food and water you offer your Canaan Dog.

PHOTO COURTESY OF MIKKI PET PRODUCTS.

Finding a good breeder, visiting the litter and selecting the perfect pup are the steps that lead up to that exciting day when your pup comes home with you!

TIME TO GO HOME

Breeders rarely release puppies until they are eight to ten weeks of age. This is an acceptable age for most breeds of dog, excepting toy breeds, which are not released until around 12 weeks, given their petite sizes. If a breeder has a puppy that is 12 weeks of age or older, it is likely well social-ized and house-trained. Be sure that it is otherwise healthy before deciding to take it home.

PUPPY-PROOFING YOUR HOME

Aside from making sure that your Canaan Dog will be comfortable in your home, you also have to make sure that your home is safe for your Canaan Dog. This means taking precau-tions that your pup will not get into anything he should not get into and that there is nothing within his reach that may harm him should he sniff it, chew it, inspect it, etc. This probably seems obvious since, while you are primarily concerned with

your pup's safety, at the same time you do not want your belongings to be ruined. Breakables should be placed out of reach if your dog is to have full run of the house. If he is to be limited to certain places within the house, keep any potentially dangerous items in the "off-limits" areas.

An electrical cord can pose a danger should the puppy decide to taste it—and who is going to convince a pup that it would not make a great chew toy? Cords should be fastened tightly against the wall. If your dog is going to spend time in a crate, make sure that there is nothing near his crate that he can reach if he sticks his curious little nose or paws through the openings. Just as you would with a child, keep all household cleaners and chemicals where the pup cannot reach them.

CHEMICAL TOXINS

Scour your garage for potential puppy dangers. Remove weed killers, pesticides and antifreeze materials. Antifreeze is highly toxic and just a few drops can kill a puppy or an adult dog. The sweet taste attracts the animal, who will quickly consume it from the floor or pavement.

It is also important to make sure that the outside of your home is safe. Of course, your puppy should never be unsupervised, but a pup let loose in your property will want to run and explore, and he should be granted that freedom. Do not let a fence give you a false sense of security. Canaani will find a way out of your encampment, whether by digging, climbing or jumping. Agility and determination embolden the Canaan's pursuit of "freedom," and they run like the wind. The average-height fence will not deter the Canaan Dog if he feels there is good need for his being on the other side. A proper fence should be no less than 5–6 feet (152–182.3 cms) high. Be sure to repair or secure any gaps in the fence. Check the fence periodically to ensure that it is in good shape and make repairs as needed; a very determined pup may return to the same spot to "work on it" until he is able to get through.

FIRST TRIP TO THE VET
You have selected your puppy, and your home and family are ready. Now all you have to do is

PUPPY PERSONALITY
When a litter becomes available to you, choosing a pup out of all those adorable faces will not be an easy task! Sound temperament is of utmost importance, but each pup has its own personality and some may be better suited to you than others. A feisty, independent pup will do well in a home with older children and adults, while quiet, shy puppies will thrive in a home with minimal noise and distractions. Your breeder knows the pups best and should be able to guide you in the right direction.

not have any problems that are not apparent to you. The vet will also set up a schedule for the pup's vaccinations; the breeder will inform you of which ones the pup has already received and the vet can continue from there

INTRODUCTION TO THE FAMILY

Everyone in the house will be excited about the puppy's coming home and will want to pet him and play with him, but it is best to make the introduction low-key so as not to overwhelm the puppy. He is apprehensive already. It is the first time he has been separated from his mother and the breeder, and the ride to your home is likely to be the first time he has been in a car. The last thing you want to do is smother him, as this will only frighten him further.

According to the AKC standard, the breed is "reserved

Never underestimate what a curious pup can stick his nose into. These aspiring photographers acquaint themselves with the camera bag.

collect your Canaan Dog from the breeder and the fun begins, right? Well…not so fast. Something else you need to plan is your pup's first trip to the vet. Perhaps the breeder can recommend someone in the area who knows spitz or pariah-type dogs, or maybe you know some other experienced dog owners who can suggest a good vet. Either way, you should have an appointment arranged for your pup before you pick him up.

The pup's first visit will consist of an overall examination to make sure that the pup does

INHERIT THE MIND

In order to know whether or not a puppy will fit into your lifestyle, you need to assess his personality. A good way to do this is to interact with his parents. Your pup inherits not only his appearance but also his personality and temperament from the sire and dam. If the parents are fearful or overly aggressive, these same traits may show up in your puppy.

and aloof with strangers," which means, like the sighthound breeds, the Canaan pup does not have the outgoing temperament of a Golden Retriever or Collie puppy. This is not to say that human contact is not extremely necessary at this stage, because this is the time when a connection between the pup and his human family is formed. Gentle petting and soothing words should help console him, as well as just putting him down and letting him explore on his own (under your watchful eye, of course).

The pup may approach the family members or may busy himself with exploring for a while. Gradually, each person should spend some time with the pup, one at a time, crouching down to get as close to the pup's level as possible, letting him sniff their hands and petting him gently. He definitely needs human attention and he needs to be touched—this is how to form an immediate bond. Supervise introductions to children, ensuring that the human young ones do not grab the puppy or abuse it (unknowingly). Likewise, be watchful of your pup's first meeting with the family feline. Just remember that the pup is experiencing many things for the first time, at the same time. There are new people, new noises, new smells and new things to investi-

gate, so be gentle, be affectionate and be as comforting as you can be.

PUP'S FIRST NIGHT HOME
You have traveled home with your new charge safely in his

NATURAL TOXINS
Examine your lawn and home landscaping before bringing your puppy home. Many varieties of plants have leaves, stems or flowers that are toxic if ingested, and you can depend on a curious puppy to investigate them. Ask your vet for information on poisonous plants or research them at your library.

crate. He's been to the vet for a thorough check-up; he's been weighed, his papers have been examined and perhaps he's even been vaccinated and wormed as well. He's met the whole family, including the excited children and the less-than-happy cat. He's explored his area, his new bed, the garden and anywhere else he's been permitted. He's eaten his first meal at home and relieved himself in the proper place. He's heard lots of new sounds, smelled new people and seen more of the outside world than ever before…and that was just the first day! He's worn out and is ready for bed…or so you think!

THE RIDE HOME

Taking your dog from the breeder to your home in a car can be a very uncomfortable experience for both of you. The puppy will have been taken from his warm, friendly, safe environment and brought into a strange new environment—an environment that moves! Be prepared for loose bowels, urination, crying, whining and even fear biting. With proper love and encouragement when you arrive home, the stress of the trip should quickly disappear.

IN DUE TIME

It will take at least two weeks for your puppy to become accustomed to his new surroundings. Give him lots of love, attention, handling, frequent opportunities to relieve himself, a diet he likes to eat and a place he can call his own.

It's puppy's first night home and you are ready to say "Good night." Keep in mind that this is his first night ever to be sleeping alone. His dam and littermates are no longer at paw's length and he's a bit scared, cold and lonely. Be reassuring to your new family member, but this is not the time to spoil him and give in to his inevitable whining.

Puppies whine to let others know where they are and hopefully to get company out of it. Place your pup in his new bed or crate in his designated area and close the door. Mercifully, he may fall asleep without a peep. When the inevitable occurs, however, ignore the whining—he is fine. Be strong and keep his interest in mind. Do not allow yourself to feel guilty and visit the pup. He will fall asleep eventually.

Many breeders recommend placing a piece of bedding from the pup's former home in his new bed so that he recognizes and is comforted by the scent of his littermates. Others still advise placing a hot water bottle in the bed for warmth. The latter may be a good idea provided the pup doesn't attempt to suckle—he'll get good and wet, and may not fall asleep so fast.

Puppy's first night can be somewhat stressful for both the pup and his new family. Remember that you are setting the tone of night-time at your house. Unless you want to play with your pup every night at 10 p.m., midnight and 2 a.m., don't initiate the habit. Your family will thank you, and so will your pup!

PREVENTING PUPPY PROBLEMS

SOCIALIZATION

Now that you have done all of the preparatory work and have helped your pup get accustomed to his new home and family, it is about time for you to have some fun! Socializing your Canaan Dog pup gives you the opportunity to show off your new friend—likely you will be the first person on your block with such an intriguing rare breed—and your pup gets to reap the benefits of being an adorable furry creature that people will want to pet and, in

general, think is absolutely precious! Do not rush your Canaan in the socialization process. Let him meet people at his own pace.

Besides getting to know his new family, your puppy should be exposed to other people,

"My littermate's ear is as good as any chew toy!" Play-biting and games among siblings are important lessons in being a dog.

MANNERS MATTER

During the socialization process, a puppy should meet people, experience different environments and definitely be exposed to other canines. Through playing and interacting with other dogs, your puppy will learn lessons, ranging from controlling the pressure of his jaws by biting his littermates to the inner-workings of the canine pack that he will apply to his human relationships for the rest of his life. That is why removing a puppy from his litter too early (before eight weeks) can be detrimental to the pup's development.

animals and situations. This will help him become well adjusted as he grows up and less prone to being timid or fearful of the new things he will encounter. Of course, he must not come into close contact with dogs you don't know well until his course of injections is fully complete.

Your pup's socialization began with the breeder, but now it is your responsibility to continue it. The socialization he receives until the age of 12 weeks is the most critical, as this is the time when he forms his impressions of the outside world. Be especially careful during the eight-to-ten-week-old period, also known as the fear period. The interaction he receives during this time should be gentle and reassuring. Lack of socialization, and/or negative experiences during the socialization period, can manifest itself in fear and aggression as the dog grows up. Your puppy needs lots of positive interaction, which of course includes human contact, affection, handling and exposure to other animals.

Once your pup has received his necessary vaccinations, feel free to take him out and about (on his lead, of course). Walk him around the neighborhood, take him on your daily errands, let people pet him, let him meet other dogs and pets, etc. Puppies do not have to try to make

> **PROPER SOCIALIZATION**
> The socialization period for puppies is from age 8 to 12 weeks. This is the time when puppies need to leave their birth family and take up residence with their new owners, where they will meet many new people, other pets, etc. Failure to be adequately socialized can cause the dog to grow up fearing others and being shy and unfriendly due to a lack of self-confidence.

friends; there will be no shortage of people who will want to introduce themselves. Just make sure that you carefully supervise each meeting. If the neighborhood children want to say hello, remember that in most cases children and pups make great companions. However, sometimes an excited child can unintentionally handle a pup too roughly, or an overzealous pup can playfully nip a little too hard. You want to make socialization experiences positive ones. What a pup learns during this very formative stage will affect his attitude toward future encounters. You want your dog to be comfortable around everyone. A pup that has a bad experience with a child may grow up to be a dog that is shy around or aggressive toward children.

CONSISTENCY IN TRAINING
Dogs, being pack animals, naturally need a leader, or else

they try to establish dominance in their packs. When you welcome a dog into your family, the choice of who becomes the leader and who becomes the "pack" is entirely up to you! Your pup's intuitive quest for dominance, coupled with the fact that it is nearly impossible to look at an adorable Canaan pup with his floppy puppy-dog ears and not cave in, give the pup almost an unfair advantage in getting the upper hand! A pup will definitely test the waters to see what he can and cannot do. Do not give in to that pleading expression—stand your ground when it comes to disciplining the pup and make sure that all family members do the same. It will only confuse the pup if Mother tells him to get off the sofa when he is used to sitting up there with Father to watch the nightly news. Avoid discrepancies by having all members of the

What's a little roughhousing among friends? This is a well-socialized pair, and the Canaan Dog doesn't mind a playful tussle with his Tibetan Spaniel companion.

household decide on the rules before the pup even comes home...and be consistent in enforcing them! Early training shapes the dog's personality, so you cannot be unclear in what you expect.

COMMON PUPPY PROBLEMS

The best way to prevent puppy problems is to be proactive in stopping an undesirable behavior as soon as it starts. The old saying "You can't teach an old dog new tricks" does not necessarily hold true, but it is true that it is much easier to discourage bad behavior in a young developing pup than to wait until the pup's bad behavior becomes the adult dog's bad habit. There are some problems that are especially prevalent in puppies as they develop.

SOCIALIZATION TIPS

Thorough socialization includes not only meeting new people but also being introduced to new experiences such as riding in the car, having his coat brushed, hearing the television, walking in a crowd—the list is endless. The more your pup experiences, and the more positive the experiences are, the less of a shock and the less frightening it will be for your pup to encounter new things.

CHEWING TIPS

Chewing goes hand in hand with nipping in the sense that a teething puppy is always looking for a way to soothe his aching gums. In this case, instead of chewing on you, he may have taken a liking to your favorite shoe or something else on which he should not be chewing. Again, realize that this is a normal canine behavior that does not need to be discouraged, only redirected. Your pup just needs to be taught what is acceptable to chew on and what is off-limits. Consistently tell him "No!" when you catch him chewing on something forbidden and give him a chew toy.

Conversely, praise him when you catch him chewing on something appropriate. In this way you are discouraging the inappropriate behavior and reinforcing the desired behavior. The puppy chewing should stop after his adult teeth have come in, but an adult dog continues to chew for various reasons—perhaps because he is bored, needs to relieve tension or just likes to chew. That is why it is important to redirect his chewing when he is still young.

NIPPING

As puppies start to teethe, they feel the need to sink their teeth into anything available...unfortunately, that usually includes your fingers, arms, hair and toes. You may find this behavior cute for the first five seconds...until you feel just how sharp those puppy teeth are. Nipping is something you want to discourage immediately and consistently with a firm "No!" (or whatever number of firm "Nos" it takes for him to understand that you mean business). Then, replace your finger with an appropriate chew toy. While this behavior is merely annoying when the dog is young, it can become dangerous as your Canaan Dog's adult teeth grow in and his jaws develop, and he continues to think it is okay to gnaw on human appendages. Your Canaan does not mean any harm with a friendly nip, but he also does not know his own strength.

CRYING/WHINING

Your pup will often cry, whine, whimper, howl or make some type of commotion when he is left alone. This is basically his

TRAINING TIP

Training your puppy takes much patience and can be frustrating at times, but you should see results from your efforts. If you have a puppy that seems untrainable, take him to a trainer or behaviorist. The dog may have a personality problem that requires the help of a professional, or perhaps you need help in learning how to train your dog.

way of calling out for attention to make sure that you know he is there and that you have not forgotten about him. Your puppy feels insecure when he is left alone, when you are out of the house and he is in his crate or when you are in another part of the house and he cannot see you. The noise he is making is an expression of the anxiety he feels at being alone, so he needs to be taught that being alone is okay. You are not actually training the dog to stop making noise; rather, you are training him to feel comfortable when he is alone and thus removing the need for him to make the noise.

This is where the crate with cozy bedding and a toy comes in handy. You want to know that your pup is safe when you are not there to supervise, and you know that he will be safe in his crate rather than roaming freely about the house. In order for the pup to stay in his crate without making a fuss, he first needs to be comfortable in his crate. On that note, it is extremely important that the crate is never used as a form of punishment; this will cause the pup to view the crate as a negative place, rather than as a place of his own for safety and retreat.

Accustom the pup to the crate in short, gradually increasing time intervals in which you put him in the crate, maybe with a treat, and stay in the room with him. If he cries or makes a fuss, do not go to him, but stay in his sight. Gradually he will realize that staying in his crate is all right without your help, and it will not be so traumatic for him when you are not around. You may want to leave the radio on softly when you leave the house; the sound of human voices may be comforting to him.

PUPPY PROBLEMS

The majority of problems that are commonly seen in young pups will disappear as your dog gets older. However, how you deal with problems when he is young will determine how he reacts to discipline as an adult dog. It is important to establish who is boss (hopefully it will be you!) right away when you are first bonding with your dog. This bond will set the tone for the rest of your life together.

HOW TO FEED YOUR CANAAN DOG

"How difficult could it be to feed a dog that derives from scavengers?" you ask. Feeding any dog in our modern society is quite simple, though it appears complicated given the vast number of options pet shops offer to dog owners. A premium dog food, the kind sold in pet shops as opposed to grocery stores, is the best choice for a Canaan Dog. This is a carnivore through and through, and the dog needs a high-quality source of protein. Breeders recommend seeking out brands where vitamin E (tocopherols) are used as the preservative, so as to avoid chemical preservatives.

Every Canaan Dog breeder should have his own tried-and-true method of feeding. Before your puppy leaves the breeder's home or kennel, you can be assured that you will depart with careful instructions on how to follow the breeder's established feeding program. In the highly unlikely case of the breeder's not automatically providing you with this information, do not leave without asking for it.

What and when you should feed your new puppy will be included in the diet sheet and it is important to understand that a specific feeding schedule is important to the puppy's well-being. A good rule of thumb for establishing intake is the amount of food that the puppy, or adult

FOOD STORAGE

You must store your dry dog food carefully. Open packages of dog food quickly lose their vitamin value, usually within 90 days of being opened. Mold spores and vermin could also contaminate the food.

for that matter, will eat in five minutes. Scavengers tend to eat quickly—so your Canaan may need a lesson in table manners to slow him down.

After weaning and up to about three months of age, the Canaan puppy should be getting three to four meals a day. At that point, two to three meals a day are sufficient, and by the time the puppy is six months old he might well be put on a morning/evening schedule. Here again, these are simply guidelines. The lean and leggy puppy might need a supplemental feeding added to the morning/evening schedule. The too-pudgy puppy should be kept on the two-meal schedule, but perhaps be given a bit less at each meal.

Most commercial foods manufactured for dogs meet nutrition standards and list the ingredients contained in the food on every package and container. The ingredients are listed in descending order, with the main ingredient listed first. Refined sugars are not a part of a canine's natural food acquisition and canine teeth are not genetically disposed to handling these sugars. Do not feed your Canaan sugar products and avoid food products that contain sugar in any high degree.

Fresh water and a properly prepared, balanced diet, containing the essential nutrients in

FOOD PREFERENCE

Selecting the best dry dog food is difficult. There is no majority consensus among veterinary scientists as to the value of nutrient analyses (protein, fat, fiber, moisture, ash, cholesterol, minerals, etc.). All agree that feeding trials are what matter most, but you also have to consider the individual dog. The dog's weight, age and activity level, and what pleases his taste, all must be considered. It is probably best to take the advice of your vet. Every dog's dietary requirements vary, even during the lifetime of a particular dog.

Consult your vet or breeder before adding supplements of meat or vegetables to the dry food. Dogs do appreciate a little variety in their diets, so you may choose to stay with the same brand but vary the flavor. Alternatively, you may wish to add a little flavored stock to give a difference to the taste.

correct proportions, are all a healthy Canaan needs to be offered. Dog foods come canned, dry, semi-moist, "scientifically fortified" and "all-natural." A visit to your local pet store will reveal how vast an array you will be able to select from.

All dogs, whether large or small, are carnivorous (meat-eating) animals. Animal proteins and fats are essential to the well-being of your Canaan Dog. However, a diet too high in proteins can lead to problems as well. Not all dry foods contain the correct amount of protein that a Canaan should have for the breed's well-being. It is best to discuss this with the breeder from whom you purchase your

dog or with your vet. The domesticated dog's diet must include protein, carbohydrates, fats, roughage and small amounts of essential minerals and vitamins. Many breeders strongly recommend adding small amounts of cooked vegetables to a Canaan's diet. This provides the necessary carbohydrates,

TEST FOR PROPER DIET

A good test for proper diet is the color, odor and firmness of your dog's stool. A healthy dog usually produces three semi-hard stools per day. The stools should have no unpleasant odor. They should be the same color from excretion to excretion.

"DOES THIS COLLAR MAKE ME LOOK FAT?"

While humans may obsess about how they look and how trim their bodies are, many people believe that extra weight on their dogs is a good thing. The truth is, pets should not be over- or under-weight, as both can lead to or signal sickness. In order to tell how fit your pet is, run your hands over his ribs. Are his ribs buried under a layer of fat or are they sticking out considerably? If your pet is within his normal weight range, you should be able to feel the ribs easily, but they should not protrude abnormally. If you stand above him, the outline of his body should resemble an hourglass. Some breeds do tend to be leaner while some are a bit stockier, but making sure your dog is the right weight for his breed will certainly contribute to his good health.

minerals and nutrients present only in vegetables.

When selecting your dog's diet, three stages of development must be considered: the puppy stage, the adult stage and the senior or veteran stage.

PUPPY STAGE

Puppies instinctively want to suck milk from their mother's teats; a normal puppy will exhibit this behavior just a few moments following birth. If puppies do not attempt to suckle within the first half-hour or so, they should be encouraged to do so by placing them on the nipples, having selected ones with plenty of milk. This early milk supply is important in providing the essential colostrum, which protects the puppies during the first eight to ten weeks of their lives. Although a mother's milk is much better than any milk formula, despite there being some excellent ones available, if the puppies do not feed, the breeder will have to feed them by hand. For those with less experience, advice from a vet is important so that not only the right quantity of milk is fed but also that of correct quality, fed at suitably frequent intervals, usually every two hours during the first few days of life.

Puppies should be allowed to nurse from their mothers for about the first six weeks, although, starting around the third or fourth week, the breeder will begin to introduce small portions of suitable solid food. Most breeders like to introduce alternate milk and meat meals initially, building up to weaning time.

By the time the puppies are seven or a maximum of eight weeks old, they should be fully weaned and fed solely on a proprietary puppy food. Selection of the most suitable, good-quality diet at this time is essential, for a

FEEDING TIPS

Dog food must be at room temperature, neither too hot nor too cold. Fresh water, changed daily and served in a clean bowl, is mandatory, especially when feeding dry food.

Never feed your dog from the table while you are eating, and never feed your dog leftovers from your own meal. They usually contain too much fat and too much seasoning.

Dogs must chew their food. Hard pellets are excellent; soups and stews are to be avoided. Don't add any extras to normal dog food without the advise of your vet. The normal food is usually balanced, and adding something extra may destroy the balance.

Except for age-related changes, dogs do not require dietary variations. They can be fed the same diet, day after day, without becoming ill.

puppy's fastest growth rate is during the first year of life. Vets are usually able to offer advice in this regard. As discussed, the frequency of meals will be reduced over time, and when a young dog has reached the age of about 12 months an adult diet should be fed. Puppy and junior diets should be well balanced for the needs of your dog so that, except in certain circumstances, additional vitamins, minerals and proteins will not be required.

ADULT DIETS

A dog is considered an adult when he has stopped growing, so in general the diet of a Canaan can be changed to an adult dog food at about 12 months of age. Again you should rely upon your vet, breeder or dietary specialist to recommend an acceptable maintenance diet. Major dog-food manufacturers specialize in this type of food, and it is merely necessary for you to select the one best suited to your dog's needs. Active dogs have different requirements than sedate dogs.

SENIOR DIETS

As dogs get older, their metabolism changes. The older dog usually exercises less, moves more slowly and sleeps more. This change in lifestyle and physiological performance requires a change in diet. Since these changes take place slowly,

A Worthy Investment

Veterinary studies have proven that a balanced high-quality diet pays off in your dog's coat quality, behavior and activity level. Invest in premium brands for the maximum payoff with your dog.

CHANGE IN DIET

As your dog's caretaker, you know the importance of keeping his diet consistent, but sometimes when you run out of food or if you're on vacation, you have to make a change quickly. Some dogs will experience digestive problems, but most will not. If you are planning on changing your dog's menu, do so gradually to ensure that your dog will not have any problems. Over a period of four to five days, slowly add some new food to your dog's regular food, increasing the percentage of new food each day.

No matter how well the family dogs get along, each should always have his own food and water bowls to ensure peaceful mealtimes where every dog gets his share.

they might not be recognizable. What is easily recognizable is weight gain. By continuing to feed your dog an adult-maintenance diet when he is slowing down metabolically, your dog will gain weight. Obesity in an older dog compounds the health problems that already accompany old age.

As your dog gets older, few of his organs function up to par. The kidneys slow down and the intestines become less efficient. These age-related factors are best handled with a change in diet and a change in feeding schedule to give smaller portions that are more easily digested. There is no single best diet for every older dog. While many dogs do well on light or senior diets, other dogs do better on puppy diets or other special premium diets such as lamb and rice. Be sensitive to your senior Canaan's diet, as this will help control other problems that may arise with your old friend.

EXERCISE

Daily exercise is an absolute must for a Canaan Dog. Most experienced owners recommend two brisk walks every day, approximately 15 minutes in length. If your schedule only permits one

EXERCISE ALERT!

You should be careful where you exercise your dog. Many countryside areas have been sprayed with chemicals that are highly toxic to both dogs and humans.

DRINK, DRANK, DRUNK—MAKE IT A DOUBLE

In both humans and dogs, as well as other living organisms, water forms the major part of nearly every body tissue. Naturally, we take water for granted, but without it, life as we know it would cease.

For dogs, water is needed to keep their bodies functioning biochemically. Additionally, water is needed to replace the water lost while panting. Unlike humans, who are able to sweat to dissipate heat, dogs must pant to cool down, thereby losing the vital water from their bodies need to regulate their body temperatures. Humans lose electrolyte-containing products and other body-fluid components through sweating; dogs do not lose anything except water.

Water is essential always, but especially so when the weather is hot or humid or when your dog is exercising or working vigorously.

good condition.

Establish a routine with your Canaan Dog. He will learn to appreciate structure and will look forward to the schedule you devise. You may find your Canaan is less enthusiastic about physical activity in the middle of the day. This is common with most dogs that like to sleep during the peak sun hours, a natural survival trait. Don't fight Nature—plan your sessions in the morning and the evening.

This is a most versatile and agile breed of dog, and owners can take advantage of the Canaan's natural abilities. With patience and skill, you can teach your Canaan to participate in formal competitions or informal matches. Agility, herding, tracking and obedience are the most popular.

WALKING LIKE A PRO

For many people, it is difficult to imagine putting their dog's well-being in someone else's hands, but if you are unable to give your dog his necessary exercise breaks, hiring a professional dog walker may be a good idea. Dog walkers offer your dog exercise, a chance to work off energy and companionship—all things that keep your dog healthy. Seek referrals from your veterinarian, breeder or groomer to find a reputable dog walker.

walk per day, it should be at least 20 to 25 minutes long. Canaani tend to keep themselves busy when playing in the yard or garden and will welcome simple games of fetch or chase. The Canaan runs very fast but fortunately tires out much faster than a sighthound like a Greyhound or Whippet would. A vigorous run with his owner will give the Canaan the physical stimulation he needs to stay in

Your Canaan Dog requires relatively little grooming, but you will need some basic grooming tools to maintain your dog's coat in healthy condition.

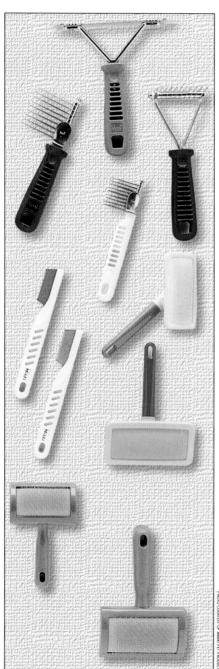

PHOTO COURTESY OF MIKKI PET PRODUCTS.

GROOMING EQUIPMENT

How much grooming equipment you purchase will depend on how much grooming you are going to do. Here are some basics:

- Natural bristle brush
- Slicker or pin brush
- Metal comb
- Rubber mat
- Dog shampoo
- Spray hose attachment
- Towels
- Ear cleaner
- Cotton balls or wipes
- Nail clippers

GROOMING

BRUSHING

The Canaan is a natural breed that requires no fancy clipping or trimming. The dogs in the States do not have coats as thick as the dogs in Israel and thus require less regular grooming. All Canaani have double coats, which means the softer undercoat will shed twice a year. To groom the Canaan, you need a good strong slicker or pin brush and a good natural bristle brush that has some nylon bristles inserted in it. You will also need a steel comb to remove any debris that collects in the longer furnishings. A comb that has teeth divided between fine and coarse is ideal.

All of these supplies are available at the local pet shop.

Regular thorough brushing with the slicker or pin brush helps keep the hair deposits on your carpeting and furniture down to a minimum. This procedure becomes an absolute necessity during those twice-a-year seasonal coat sheddings. There's no need to tell you what times of the year your Canaan will blow his coat. Your regular brushing will tell you that in a hurry. Or, if you fall behind on your brushing chores, the clouds of coat floating through the house will quickly inform you.

When brushing, proceed vigorously from behind the head to that famous bushy tail. Do this all over the body and be especially careful to attend to the hard-to-reach areas between the legs, behind the ears and under the body. Mats can occur, particularly when the dog is shedding or when the coat catches burrs or sticky substances in the longer furnishings.

Should you encounter a mat that does not brush out easily, use your fingers and the steel comb to separate the hairs as much as possible. Do not cut or pull out the matted hair. Apply baby powder or one of the specially prepared grooming powders directly to the mat and brush completely from the skin out.

Follow your hair-slicker or pin brushing with a stimulating brushing with the bristle brush. Together, these will keep both the coat and skin clean and healthy.

BATHING

You can dry-bathe your Canaan by sprinkling a little baby powder in the coat and then working it well in and brushing it out. This, of course, also helps to make the dog smell good. Over-bathing can lead to dry skin

Routine brushing, combing and the occasional bath are all that are needed to care for the Canaan Dog's coat.

The Canaan's hair is longest on the bushy tail; brushing avoids the tail's tangling and keeps it looking full.

problems. Dry skin creates a need to scratch and this can lead to severe scratching and hot spots, which are moist sore areas in which the coat is entirely scratched or bitten away.

There will be times when your Canaan Dog will require a good old-fashioned bath. Again, like most anything, if you

A metal comb is helpful for removing any debris from the coat.

A strong pin brush removes dead hair; this is especially important during shedding seasons, when you'd rather have the hair in the brush than all over the house!

accustom your pup to being bathed as a puppy, it will be second nature by the time he grows up. You want your dog to be at ease in the bath or else it could end up a wet, soapy, messy ordeal for both of you!

Brush your Canaan thoroughly before wetting his coat. This will get rid of most mats and tangles, which are harder to remove when the coat is wet. Make certain that your dog has a good non-slip surface on which to stand. Begin by wetting the dog's coat, checking the water temperature to make sure that it is neither too hot nor too cold. A shower or hose attachment is necessary for thoroughly wetting and rinsing the coat.

BATHING BEAUTY

Once you are sure that the dog is thoroughly rinsed, squeeze the excess water out of his coat with your hand and dry him with a heavy towel. You may choose to use a blow dryer on a low setting or just let the coat dry naturally. In cold weather, never allow your dog outside with a wet coat.

There are "dry bath" products on the market, which are sprays and powders intended for spot cleaning, that can be used between regular baths if necessary. They are not substitutes for regular baths, but they are easy to use for touch-ups as they do not require rinsing.

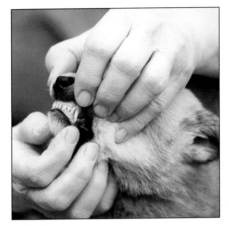

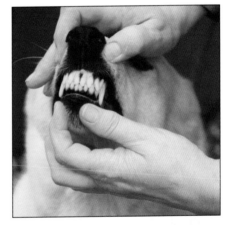

Accustom your puppy to having his teeth brushed and initiate a home dental-care regimen that will be a part of your Canaan Dog's routine care throughout his life. Above: a healthy puppy bite. Below: a healthy adult bite.

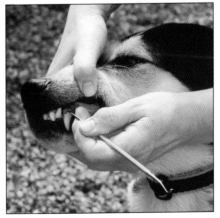

Tooth scaling is more difficult than the routine tooth-brushing you'll do with your Canaan Dog. Your vet can either scale your dog's teeth or show you how to do it properly.

The outer part of the ear can be cleaned with a soft wipe. Never enter the ear canal.

Special ear liquid or powder is available where you buy pet supplies. It assists in keeping the ear clean and parasite-free.

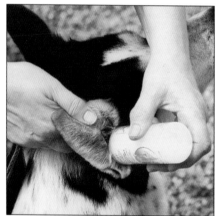

A soft wipe also is used around the eyes to clean any dirt build-up or tear stains. Tear-stain remover is available from most pet shops.

Next, apply shampoo to the dog's coat and work it into a good lather. Wash the head last, as you do not want shampoo to drip into the dog's eyes while you are washing the rest of his body. You should use only a shampoo that is made for dogs. Do not use a product made for human hair. Work the shampoo all the way down to the skin. You can use this opportunity to check the skin for any bumps, bites or other abnormalities. Do not neglect any area of the body—get all of the hard-to-reach places.

Once the dog has been thoroughly shampooed, he requires an equally thorough rinsing. Shampoo left in the coat can be irritating to the dog's skin. Protect his eyes from the shampoo by shielding them with your hand and directing the flow of water in the opposite direction. You should also avoid getting water in the ear canal. Be prepared for your dog to shake out his coat—you might want to stand back, but make sure you have a hold on the dog to keep him from running through the house.

NAIL TRIMMING

Use grooming times to accustom your Canaan to having his nails trimmed and feet inspected. Always inspect your dog's feet for cracked pads. Check between the toes for splinters and thorns that may be embedded in the soft hair

NAIL FILING

You can purchase an electric tool to grind down a dog's nails rather than cut them. Some dogs don't seem to mind the electric grinder but will object strongly to nail clippers. Talking it over with your veterinarian will help you make the right choice.

PEDICURE TIP

A dog that spends a lot of time outside on a hard surface, such as cement or pavement, will have his nails naturally worn down and may not need to have them trimmed as often, except maybe in the colder months when he is not outside as much. Regardless, it is best to get your dog accustomed to the nail-trimming procedure at an early age so that he is used to it. Some dogs are especially sensitive about having their feet touched, but if a dog has experienced it since puppyhood, it should not bother him.

between the pads and toes. Pay particular attention to any swollen or tender areas.

We suggest attending to your dog's nails at intervals of about every three weeks and certainly no longer than four weeks. Long nails spread and weaken the foot. The nails of a Canaan that isn't exercising on rough terrain will grow long very quickly.

Each nail has a blood vessel called the "quick" running through the center. The quick grows close to the end of the nail and contains very sensitive nerve endings. If the nail is allowed to grow too long, it will be impossible to cut it back to a proper length without cutting into the quick. This causes severe pain to the dog and can also result in a great deal of bleeding that can be very difficult to stop.

Nails can be trimmed with canine nail clippers or an electric nail grinder called a drummel. Use the "fine" grinding disc on the drummel because this allows you to trim back the nail a little

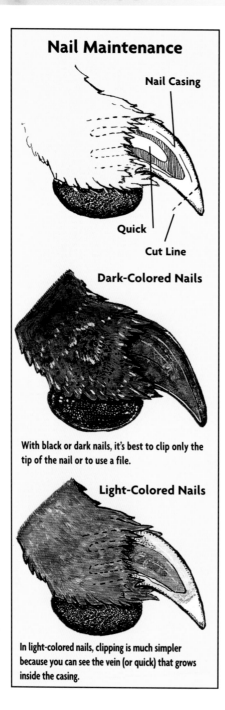

Nail Maintenance

Nail Casing

Quick

Cut Line

Dark-Colored Nails

With black or dark nails, it's best to clip only the tip of the nail or to use a file.

Light-Colored Nails

In light-colored nails, clipping is much simpler because you can see the vein (or quick) that grows inside the casing.

bit at a time, practically eliminating the risk of any bleeding.

Always proceed with caution and remove only a small portion of the nail at a time. Should the quick be nipped in the trimming process, there are a number of blood-clotting products available at pet shops that will almost immediately stem the flow of blood. You can also use a styptic pencil, such as the type used for shaving. It is wise to have one of these products on hand anyway in case your dog breaks a nail in some way.

TRAVELING WITH YOUR DOG

CAR TRAVEL

You should accustom your Canaan to riding in a car at an early age. You may or may not take him in the car often, but at the very least he will need to go to the vet and you do not want these trips to be traumatic for the dog or troublesome for you. The safest way for a dog to ride in the car is in his crate. If he uses a crate in the house, you can use the same crate for travel. Another option for car travel is a specially made safety harness for dogs, which straps the dog in much like a seat belt. Do not let the dog roam loose in the vehicle—this is very dangerous! If you should stop short, your dog can be thrown and injured. If the dog

TRAVEL TIP
Never leave your dog alone in the car. In hot weather, your dog can die from the high temperature inside a closed vehicle; even a car parked in the shade can heat up very quickly. Leaving the window open is dangerous as well since the dog can hurt himself trying to get out.

ON-LEAD ONLY
When traveling, never let your dog off-lead in a strange area. Your dog could run away out of fear, decide to chase a passing squirrel or cat or simply want to stretch his legs without restriction—if any of these happen, you might never see your canine friend again.

starts climbing on you and pestering you while you are driving, you will not be able to concentrate on the road. It is an unsafe situation for everyone—human and canine.

For long trips, be prepared to stop to let the dog relieve himself. Take with you whatever you need to clean up after him, including some paper towels and

GOING ABROAD
For international travel, you will have to make arrangements well in advance (perhaps months), as countries' regulations pertaining to bringing in animals differ. There may be special health certificates and/or vaccinations that your dog will need before taking the trip; sometimes this has to be done within a certain time frame. When traveling to rabies-free countries, you will need to bring proof of the dog's rabies vaccination and there will likely be a quarantine period upon arrival.

perhaps some old bath towels for use should he have an accident in the car or suffer from motion sickness.

Air Travel
Contact your chosen airline before proceeding with travel plans that include your Canaan. The dog will be required to travel in a fiberglass crate and you should always check in advance with the airline about specific requirements regarding the crate's size, type and labeling. To help put the dog at ease, give him one of his favorite toys in the crate. Do not feed the dog for several hours prior to checking in so that you minimize his need to relieve himself. However, certain regulations may specify that food and water bowls, and a portion of food, must be attached to the crate.

Make sure your dog is properly identified and that your contact information appears on his ID tags and on his crate.

IDENTIFICATION OPTIONS

As puppies become more and more expensive, especially those puppies of high quality for showing and/or breeding, they have a greater chance of being stolen. The usual collar dog tag is, of course, easily removed. But there are two more permanent techniques that have become widely used for identification.

The puppy microchip implantation involves the injection of a small microchip, about the size of a corn kernel, under the skin of the dog. If your dog shows up at a clinic or shelter, or is offered for resale under less-than-savory circumstances, it can be positively identified by the microchip. The microchip is scanned, and a registry quickly identifies you as the owner.

Tattooing is done on various parts of the dog, from his belly to his cheeks. The number tattooed can be your telephone number or any other number that you can easily memorize. When professional dog thieves see a tattooed dog, they usually lose interest. For the safety of our dogs, no laboratory facility or dog broker will accept a tattooed dog as stock. Both microchipping and tattooing can be done at your local veterinary clinic.

Animals travel in a different area of the plane than human passengers, so every rule must be strictly followed so as to prevent the risk of getting separated from your dog.

VACATIONS AND BOARDING

So you want to take a family vacation—and you want to include *all* members of the family. You would probably make arrangements for accommodations ahead of time anyway, but this is especially important when traveling with a dog. You do not want to make an overnight stop at the only place around for miles, only to find out that they do not allow dogs. Also, you do not want to reserve a place for your family without

confirming that you are traveling with a dog, because, if it is against their policy, you may end up without a place to stay.

Alternatively, if you are traveling and choose not to bring your Canaan, you will have to make arrangements for him while you are away. Some options are to take him to a neighbor's house to stay while you are gone, to have a trusted

LOST AND FOUND

You have a valuable dog. If the dog is lost or stolen, you would undoubtedly become extremely upset. Likewise, if you encounter a lost dog, notify the police or the local animal shelter.

neighbor take the dog to his home or stay at your house or to bring your dog to a reputable boarding kennel. If you choose to board him at a kennel, you should visit in advance to see the facilities provided and where the dogs are kept. Are the dogs' areas spacious and kept clean? Talk to some of the employees and observe how they treat the dogs—do they spend time with the dogs, play with them, exercise them, etc.? Also find out the kennel's policy on vaccinations and what they require. This is for all of the dogs' safety, since there is a greater risk of diseases being passed from dog to dog when dogs are kept together.

IDENTIFICATION

Your Canaan Dog is your valued companion and friend. That is why you always keep a close eye on him and you have made sure that he cannot escape from the garden or wriggle out of his collar and run away from you. However, accidents can happen and there may come a time when your dog unexpectedly becomes separated from you. If this unfortunate event should occur, the first thing on your mind will be finding him. Proper identification, including an ID tag, a tattoo and possibly a microchip, will increase the chances of your Canaan Dog's being returned to you safely and quickly.

Your Canaan Dog should always wear his identification tags on his collar, even if he is microchipped or tattooed. The collar tells anyone who finds him that he is someone's pet, and the tags give your contact information to help ensure his return to you.

TRAINING YOUR
CANAAN DOG

Living with an untrained dog is a lot like owning a piano that you do not know how to play—it is a nice object to look at, but it does not do much more than that to bring you pleasure. Now try taking piano lessons, and suddenly the piano comes alive and brings forth magical sounds and rhythms that set your heart singing and your body swaying.

The same is true with your Canaan Dog. Any dog is a big responsibility and, if not trained sensibly, may develop unacceptable behavior that annoys you or could even cause family friction.

To train your Canaan, you may like to enroll in an obedience class. Teach your dog good manners as you learn how and why he behaves the way he does. Find out how to communicate with your dog and how to recognize and understand his communications with you. Suddenly the dog takes on a new role in your life—he is clever, interesting, well behaved and fun to be with. He demonstrates his bond of devotion to you daily. In other words, your Canaan does wonders for your ego because he constantly reminds you that you are not only his leader, you are his hero!

Those involved with teaching dog obedience and counseling owners about their dogs' behavior have discovered some interesting facts about dog ownership. For example, training dogs when they are puppies results in the highest rate of success in developing well-mannered and well-adjusted adult dogs. Training an older dog, from six months to six years of age, can produce almost equal results, providing that the owner accepts the dog's slower rate of learning capability and is willing to work patiently to help the dog succeed at developing to his fullest potential. Unfortunately, many owners of untrained adult dogs lack the patience factor, so they do not persist until their dogs are successful at learning particular behaviors.

Training a puppy aged 10 to 16 weeks (20 weeks at the most) is like working with a dry sponge in a pool of water. The pup soaks up whatever you show him and constantly looks for more things to do and learn. At this early age,

One of the most important endeavors in training your Canaan is house-training. Relief behaviors differ between males (top), who usually lift their legs, and females (bottom), who squat.

Make an impression on your pup at a young age. As Canaani are not very far removed from their feral origins, the earlier the training starts, the better.

his body is not yet producing hormones, and therein lies the reason for such a high rate of success. Without hormones, he is focused on his owners and not particularly interested in investigating other places, dogs, people, etc. You are his leader: his provider of food, water, shelter and security. He latches onto you and wants to stay close. He will usually follow you from room to room, will not let you out of his sight when you are outdoors with him and will respond in like manner to the people and animals you encounter. If you greet a friend warmly, he will be willing to greet the person as well. If, however, you are hesitant or anxious about the approach of a stranger, he will respond accordingly.

Once the puppy begins to produce hormones, his natural curiosity emerges and he begins to investigate the world around him. It is at this time when you may notice that the untrained dog begins to wander away from you and even ignore your commands to stay close. When this behavior becomes a problem, you have two choices: get rid of the dog or train him. It is strongly urged that you choose the latter option.

You usually will be able to find obedience classes within a reasonable distance from your home, but you can also do a lot to train your dog yourself. Sometimes there are classes available, but the tuition is too costly. Whatever the circumstances, the solution to training your dog without obedience classes lies within the pages of this book.

This chapter is devoted to helping you train your Canaan Dog at home. If the recommended

REAP THE REWARDS
If you start with a normal, healthy dog and give him time, patience and some carefully executed lessons, you will reap the rewards of that training for the life of the dog. And what a life it will be! The two of you will find immeasurable pleasure in the companionship you have built together with love, respect and understanding.

procedures are followed faithfully, you may expect positive results that will prove rewarding both to you and your dog.

Whether your new charge is a puppy or a mature adult, the methods of teaching and the techniques we use in training basic behaviors are the same. After all, no dog, whether puppy or adult, likes harsh or inhumane methods. All creatures, however, and the Canaan Dog in particular, respond favorably to gentle motivational methods and sincere praise and encouragement. Now let us get started.

HOUSE-TRAINING

The Canaan Dog is a naturally clean dog and can be house-trained with relative ease. Even young puppies exhibit clean habits from a very early age, but your involvement in the training process is key. You can train a puppy to relieve himself wherever you choose, but this must be somewhere suitable. You should bear in mind from the outset that when your puppy is old enough to go out in public places, any canine deposits must be removed at once. You will always have to carry with you a small plastic bag or "poop-scoop."

Outdoor training includes such surfaces as grass, soil and cement. Indoor training usually means training your dog to newspaper. When deciding on the surface and location that you will want your Canaan to use, be sure it is going to be permanent. Training your dog to grass and then changing your mind a few months later is extremely difficult for both dog and owner.

Next, choose the command you will use each and every time you want your puppy to void.

PARENTAL GUIDANCE
Training a dog is a life experience. Many parents admit that much of what they know about raising children they learned from caring for their dogs. Dogs respond to love, fairness and guidance, just as children do. Become a good dog owner and you may become an even better parent.

"Hurry up" and "Let's go" are examples of commands commonly used by dog owners. Get in the habit of giving the puppy your chosen relief command before you take him out. That way, when he becomes an adult, you will be able to determine if he wants to go out when you ask him. A confirmation will be signs of interest like wagging his tail, watching you intently, going to the door, etc.

PUPPY'S NEEDS

The puppy needs to relieve himself after play periods, after each meal, after he has been sleeping and at any time he indicates that he is looking for a place to urinate or defecate. The urinary and intestinal tract muscles of very young puppies are not fully developed. Therefore, like human babies, puppies need to relieve themselves frequently.

Take your puppy out often— every hour for an eight-week-old, for example—and always immediately after sleeping and eating. The older the puppy, the less often he will need to relieve himself. Finally, as a mature healthy adult, he will require only three to five relief trips per day.

HOUSING

Since the types of housing and control you provide for your puppy have a direct relationship on the success of house-training, we consider the various aspects of both before we begin training.

Taking a new puppy home and turning him loose in your house can be compared to turning a child loose in a sports arena and telling the child that the place is all his! The sheer enormity of the place would be too much for him to handle. Instead, offer the puppy clearly defined areas where he can play, sleep, eat and live. A room of the house where the family gathers is the most obvious choice. Puppies are social animals and need to feel a part of the pack right from the start. Hearing your voice, watching you while you are doing things and smelling you nearby are all positive reinforcers that he is now a member of your pack. Usually a family room, the kitchen or a nearby adjoining breakfast area is ideal for providing safety and security for both puppy and owner.

Within the designated room, there should be a smaller area that the puppy can call his own. An alcove, a wire or fiberglass dog crate or a fenced (not boarded!) corner from which he can view the activities of his new family will be fine. The size of the area or crate is the key factor here. The area must be large enough so that the puppy can lie down and stretch out, as well as stand up, without rubbing his head on the top. At the same time, it must be small enough so that he cannot

CANINE DEVELOPMENT SCHEDULE

It is important to understand how and at what age a puppy develops into adulthood. If you are a puppy owner, consult the following Canine Development Schedule to determine the stage of development your puppy is currently experiencing. This knowledge will help you as you work with the puppy in the weeks and months ahead.

Period	Age	Characteristics
FIRST TO THIRD	BIRTH TO SEVEN WEEKS	Puppy needs food, sleep and warmth, and responds to simple and gentle touching. Needs mother for security and disciplining. Needs littermates for learning and interacting with other dogs. Pup learns to function within a pack and learns pack order of dominance. Begin socializing with adults and children for short periods. Begins to become aware of its environment.
FOURTH	EIGHT TO TWELVE WEEKS	Brain is fully developed. Needs socializing with outside world. Remove from mother and littermates. Needs to change from canine pack to human pack. Human dominance necessary. Fear period occurs between 8 and 12 weeks. Avoid fright and pain.
FIFTH	THIRTEEN TO SIXTEEN WEEKS	Training and formal obedience should begin. Less association with other dogs, more with people, places, situations. Period will pass easily if you remember this is pup's change-to-adolescence time. Be firm and fair. Flight instinct prominent. Permissiveness and over-disciplining can do permanent damage. Praise for good behavior.
JUVENILE	FOUR TO EIGHT MONTHS	Another fear period about 7 to 8 months of age. It passes quickly, but be cautious of fright and pain. Sexual maturity reached. Dominant traits established. Dog should understand sit, down, come and stay by now.

NOTE: THESE ARE APPROXIMATE TIME FRAMES. ALLOW FOR INDIVIDUAL DIFFERENCES IN PUPPIES.

relieve himself at one end and sleep at the other without coming into contact with his droppings before he is fully trained to relieve himself outside. By nature, all dogs are clean animals and will not remain close to their relief areas unless forced to do so. Canaani will never sleep or eat near their relief areas.

The dog's designated area should contain clean bedding and a toy. Water must always be available, in a non-spill container, once house-training has been reliably achieved.

CONTROL

By *control*, we mean helping the puppy to create a lifestyle pattern that will be compatible to that of his human pack (YOU!). Just as we guide little children to learn our way of life, we must show the

THE SUCCESS METHOD
6 Steps to Successful Crate Training

1 Tell the puppy "Crate time!" and place him in the crate with a small treat (a piece of cheese or half of a biscuit). Let him stay in the crate for five minutes while you are in the same room. Then release him and praise lavishly. Never release him when he is fussing. Wait until he is quiet before you let him out.

2 Repeat Step 1 several times a day.

3 The next day, place the puppy in the crate as before. Let him stay there for ten minutes. Do this several times.

4 Continue building time in five-minute increments until the puppy stays in his crate for 30 minutes with you in the room. Always take him to his relief area after prolonged periods in his crate.

5 Now go back to Step 1 and let the puppy stay in his crate for five minutes, this time while you are out of the room.

6 Once again, build crate time in five-minute increments with you out of the room. When the puppy will stay willingly in his crate (he may even fall asleep!) for 30 minutes with you out of the room, he will be ready to stay in it for several hours at a time.

THE SUCCESS METHOD

Success that comes by luck is usually short-lived. Success that comes by well-thought-out proven methods is often more easily achieved and permanent. This is the Success Method. It is designed to give you, the puppy owner, a simple yet proven way to help your puppy develop clean living habits and a feeling of security in his new environment.

It's best if you pick your pup's relief area, unless you don't mind your flowerbeds' being "watered" a bit more often than necessary.

puppy when it is time to play, eat, sleep, exercise and even entertain himself.

Your puppy should always sleep in his crate. He should also learn that, during times of household confusion and excessive human activity, such as at breakfast when family members are preparing for the day, he can play by himself in relative safety and comfort in his designated

HOW MANY TIMES A DAY?

AGE	RELIEF TRIPS
To 14 weeks	10
14–22 weeks	8
22–32 weeks	6
Adulthood	4
(dog stops growing)	

These are estimates, of course, but they are a guide to the minimum number of opportunities a dog should have each day to relieve himself.

PLAN TO PLAY

The puppy should also have regular play and exercise sessions when he is with you or a family member. Exercise for a very young puppy can consist of a short walk around the house or yard. Playing can include fetching games with a large ball or a special toy. (All puppies teethe and need soft things upon which to chew.) Remember to restrict play periods to indoors within his living area (the family room, for example) until he is completely house-trained.

SAFETY FIRST

While it may seem that the most important things to your dog are eating, sleeping and chewing the upholstery on your furniture, his first concern is actually safety. The domesticated dogs we keep as companions have the same pack instinct as their ancestors who ran free thousands of years ago. Because of this pack instinct, your dog wants to know that he and his pack are not in danger of being harmed, and that his pack has a strong, capable leader. You must establish yourself as the leader early on in your relationship. That way, your dog will trust that you will take care of him and the pack, and he will accept your commands without question.

The relief schedule of very young pups is based solely on when they need to "go." These young Canaani are done with their outing and ready to come back inside.

area. Each time you leave the puppy alone, he should understand exactly where he is to stay.

Puppies are chewers. They cannot tell the difference between lamp cords, television wires, shoes, table legs, etc. Chewing into a television wire, for example, can be fatal to the puppy, while a shorted wire can start a fire in the house. If the puppy chews on the arm of the chair when he is alone, you will probably discipline him angrily when you get home. Thus, he makes the association that your coming home means he is going to be punished. (He will not remember chewing the chair and is incapable of making the association of the discipline with his

THE CLEAN LIFE

By providing sleeping and resting quarters that fit the dog, and offering frequent opportunities to relieve himself outside his quarters, the puppy quickly learns that the outdoors (or the newspaper if you are training him to paper) is the place to go when he needs to urinate or defecate. It also reinforces his innate desire to keep his sleeping quarters clean. This, in turn, helps develop the muscle control that will eventually produce a dog with clean living habits.

FEAR AGGRESSION

Pups who are subjected to physical abuse during training commonly end up with behavioral problems as adults. One common result of abuse is fear aggression, in which a dog will lash out, bare his teeth, snarl and finally bite someone by whom he feels threatened. For example, your daughter may be playing with the dog one afternoon. As they play hide-and-seek, she backs the dog into a corner and, as she attempts to tease him playfully, he bites her hand. Examine the cause of this behavior. Did your daughter ever hit the dog? Did someone who resembles your daughter hit or scream at the dog?

Fortunately, fear aggression is relatively easy to correct. Have your daughter engage in only positive activities with the dog, such as feeding, petting and walking. She should not give any corrections or negative feedback. If the dog still growls or cowers away from her, allow someone else to accompany them. After approximately one week, the dog should feel that he can rely on her for many positive things, and he will also be prevented from reacting fearfully towards anyone who might resemble her.

naughty deed.) Accustoming the pup to his designated area not only keeps him safe but also avoids his engaging in destructive behaviors when you are not around.

Times of excitement, such as special occasions, family parties, etc., can be fun for the puppy, providing that he can view the activities from the security of his designated area. He is not underfoot and he is not being fed all sorts of tidbits that will probably cause him stomach distress, yet he still feels a part of the fun.

SCHEDULE

A puppy should be taken to his relief area each time he is released from his designated area, after meals, after a play session and when he first awakens in the morning (at age eight weeks, this can mean 5 a.m.!). The puppy will indicate that he's ready "to go" by circling or sniffing busily—do not misinterpret these signs. For a puppy less than ten weeks of age, a routine of taking him out every hour is necessary. As the puppy grows, he will be able to wait for longer periods of time.

Keep trips to his relief area short. Stay no more than five or six minutes and then return to the house. If he goes during that time, praise him lavishly and take him indoors immediately. If he does not, but he has an accident when you go back indoors, pick him up immediately, say "No! No!" and return to his relief area. Wait a few minutes, then return to the house again. Never hit a puppy or rub his face in urine or excrement when he has had an accident!

Once indoors, put the puppy in his crate until you have had time to clean up his accident. Then, release him to the family area and watch him more closely than before. Chances are, his accident was a result of your not picking up his signal or waiting too long before offering him the opportunity to relieve himself. Never hold a grudge against the puppy for accidents.

Let the puppy learn that going outdoors means it is time to relieve himself, not to play. Once trained, he will be able to play indoors and out and still differentiate between the times for play versus the times for relief.

Help him develop regular hours for naps, being alone, playing by himself and just resting, all in his crate. Encourage him to entertain himself while you are busy with your activities. Let him learn that having you near is comforting, but it is not your main purpose in life to provide him with undivided attention.

Each time you put your puppy in his own area, use the same command, whatever suits best. Soon he will run to his crate or special area when he hears you say those words.

Crate training provides safety for you, the puppy and the home. It also provides the puppy with a feeling of security, and that helps the puppy achieve self-confidence and clean habits. Remember that one of the primary ingredients in house-training your puppy is control. Regardless of your lifestyle, there will always be occasions when you will need to have a place where your dog can stay and be happy and safe. Crate training is the answer for now and in the future.

In conclusion, a few key elements are really all you need for a successful house-training method—consistency, frequency, praise, control and supervision. By following these procedures with a normal, healthy puppy, you and the puppy will soon be past the stage of accidents and ready to move on to a full and rewarding life together.

ROLES OF DISCIPLINE, REWARD AND PUNISHMENT

Discipline, training one to act in accordance with rules, brings order to life. It is as simple as that. Without discipline, particularly in a group society, chaos will reign supreme and the group will eventually perish. Humans and canines are social animals and need some form of discipline in order to function effectively. They must procure food, protect their home base and their young and reproduce to keep their species going. If there were no discipline in the lives of social animals, they would eventually die from starvation and/or predation by other stronger animals.

CALM DOWN
Dogs will do anything for your attention. If you reward the dog when he is calm and attentive, you will develop a well-mannered dog. If, on the other hand, you greet your dog excitedly and encourage him to wrestle with you, the dog will greet you the same way and you will have a hyperactive dog on your hands.

In the case of domestic canines, discipline in their lives is needed in order for them to understand how their pack (you and other family members) functions and how they must act in order to survive.

A large humane society in a highly populated area recently surveyed dog owners regarding their satisfaction with their relationships with their dogs. People who had trained their dogs were 75% more satisfied with their pets than those who had never trained their dogs.

Dr. Edward Thorndike, a noted psychologist, established *Thorndike's Theory of Learning*, which states that a behavior that results in a pleasant event tends to be repeated. Likwise, a behavior that results in an unpleasant event tends not to be repeated. It is this theory upon which training methods are based today. For example, if you manipulate a dog to perform a specific behavior and reward him for doing it, he is likely to do it again because he enjoyed the end result.

Occasionally, punishment, a penalty inflicted for an offense, is necessary. The best type of punishment often comes from an outside source. For example, a child is told not to touch the oven because he may get burned. He disobeys and touches the oven. In doing so, he receives a burn. From that time on, he respects the heat of the oven and avoids contact with it. Therefore, a behavior that results in an unpleasant event tends not to be repeated.

A good example of a dog's learning the hard way is the dog who chases the house cat. He is told many times to leave the cat alone, yet he persists in teasing the cat. Then, one day, the dog begins chasing the cat but the cat turns and swipes a claw across the dog's face, leaving the dog

A young pup might find it hard to take a break from exploring to focus on a lesson, but a food treat is a sure way to get his attention.

Adult Canaani who are accustomed to their lessons are usually focused on the trainer, but this handsome guy can't resist a quick pose for the camera.

TREATS

Have a bag of treats on hand; something nutritious and easy to swallow works best. Use a soft treat, a chunk of cheese or a piece of cooked chicken rather than a dry biscuit. By the time the dog has finished chewing a dry treat, he will forget why he is being rewarded in the first place!

Using food rewards will not teach a dog to beg at the table— the only way to teach a dog to beg at the table is to give him food from the table. In training, rewarding the dog with a food treat will help him associate praise and the treats with learning new behaviors that obviously please his owner.

TRAINING BEGINS: ASK THE DOG A QUESTION

In order to teach your dog anything, you must first get his attention. After all, he cannot learn anything if he is looking away from you with his mind on something else.

To get your dog's attention, ask him "School?" and immediately walk over to him and give

with a painful gash on his nose. The final result is that the dog stops chasing the cat. Again, a behavior that results in an unpleasant event tends not to be repeated.

TRAINING EQUIPMENT

COLLAR AND LEAD

For a Canaan Dog, the collar and lead that you use for training must be one with which you are easily able to work, not too heavy for the dog and perfectly safe.

OPEN MINDS

Dogs are as different from each other as people are. What works for one dog may not work for another. Have an open mind. If one method of training is unsuccessful, try another.

him a treat as you tell him "Good dog." Wait a minute or two and repeat the routine, this time with a treat in your hand as you approach within a foot of the dog. Do not go directly to him, but stop about a foot short of him and hold out the treat as you ask "School?" He will see you approaching with a treat in your hand and most likely begin walking toward you. As you meet, give him the treat and praise again.

The third time, ask the question, have a treat in your hand and walk only a short distance toward the dog so that he must walk almost all the way to you. As he reaches you, give him the treat and praise again.

By this time, the dog will probably be getting the idea that if he pays attention to you, especially when you ask that question, it will pay off in treats and enjoyable activities for him. In other words, he learns that "school" means doing great things with you that are fun and that result in positive attention for him.

Remember that the dog does not understand your verbal language; he only recognizes sounds. Your question translates to a series of sounds for him, and those sounds become the signal to go to you and pay attention. The dog learns that if he does this, he will get to interact with you plus receive treats and praise.

THE BASIC COMMANDS

TEACHING SIT

Now that you have the dog's attention, attach his lead and hold it in your left hand, and hold a food treat in your right hand. Place your food hand at the dog's nose and let him lick the treat but not take it from you. Say "Sit" and slowly raise your food hand from in front of the dog's nose up over his head so that he is looking at the ceiling. As he bends his head upward, he will have to bend his knees to maintain his

Teaching your dog to sit is a basic exercise and the foundation of other commands, such as the sit/stay.

balance. As he bends his knees, he will assume a sit position. At that point, release the food treat and praise lavishly with comments such as "Good dog! Good sit!" Remember to always praise enthusiastically, because dogs relish verbal praise from their owners and feel so proud of themselves whenever they accomplish a behavior.

You will not use food forever in getting the dog to obey your commands. Food is only used to teach new behaviors and, once the dog knows what you want when you give a specific command, you will wean him off the food treats but still maintain the verbal praise. After all, you will always have your voice with you, and there will be many times when you have no food rewards but expect the dog to obey.

Training is more than just commands; it also includes socialization to ensure a peaceful environment among family pets. This six-week-old Canaan and adult Tibetan Spaniel see eye-to-eye now, but it won't be long before the youngster towers over his friend.

TEACHING DOWN

Teaching the down exercise is easy when you understand how the dog perceives the down position, and it is very difficult when you do not. Dogs perceive the down position as a submissive one; therefore, teaching the down exercise by using a forceful method can sometimes make the dog develop such a fear of the down that he either runs away when you say "Down" or he attempts to snap at the person who tries to force him down.

Have the dog sit close alongside your left leg, facing in the same direction as you are. Hold the lead in your left hand and a food treat in your right. Now place your left hand lightly on the top of the dog's shoulders where they meet above the spinal cord. Do not push down on the dog's shoulders; simply rest your left hand there so you can guide the dog to lie down close to your left leg rather than to swing away from your side when he drops.

Now place the food hand at the dog's nose, say "Down" very softly (almost a whisper) and slowly lower the food hand to the dog's front feet. When the food hand reaches the floor, begin moving it forward along the floor in front of the dog. Keep talking softly to the dog, saying things like, "Do you want this treat? You can do this, good dog." Your reassuring tone of voice will help calm the dog as he tries to follow the food hand in order to get the treat.

When the dog's elbows touch the floor, release the food and praise softly. Try to get the dog to maintain that down position for several seconds before you let him sit up again. The goal here is to get the dog to settle down and not feel threatened in the down position.

TEACHING STAY

It is easy to teach the dog to stay in either a sit or a down position. Again, we use food and praise during the teaching process as we help the dog to understand exactly what it is that we are expecting him to do.

To teach the sit/stay, start with the dog sitting on your left side as before and hold the lead in your left hand. Have a food treat in your right hand and place your food hand at the dog's nose. Say

DOUBLE JEOPARDY

A dog in jeopardy never lies down. He stays alert on his feet because instinct tells him that he may have to run away or fight for his survival. Therefore, if a dog feels threatened or anxious, he will not lie down. Consequently, it is important to keep the dog calm and relaxed as he learns the down exercise.

"Stay" and step out on your right foot to stand directly in front of the dog, toe to toe, as he licks and nibbles the treat. Be sure to keep his head facing upward to maintain the sit position. Count to five and then swing around to stand next to the dog again with him on your left. As soon as you get back to the original position, release the food and praise lavishly.

To teach the down/stay, do the down as previously described. As soon as the dog lies down, say "Stay" and step out on your right foot just as you did in the sit/stay. Count to five and then return to stand beside the dog with him on your left side. Release the treat and praise as always.

Within a week or ten days, you can begin to add a bit of distance between you and your dog when you leave him. When you do, use your left hand open with the palm facing the dog as a stay signal. Hold the food treat in your right hand as before, but this time the food will not be touching the dog's nose. He will watch the food hand and quickly learn that he is going to get that treat as soon as you return to his side.

When you can stand 1 yard away from your dog for 30 seconds, you can then begin building time and distance in both stays. Eventually, the dog can be expected to remain in the stay position for prolonged periods of time until you return to him or call him to you. Always praise lavishly when he stays.

TEACHING COME

If you make teaching "come" an exciting experience, you should never have a student that does not love the game or that fails to come when called. The secret, it seems, is never to use the word "come."

At times when an owner most wants his dog to come when called, the owner is likely to be upset or anxious and he allows these feelings to come through in the tone of his voice when he calls his dog. Hearing that desperation in his owner's voice, the dog fears the results of going to him and therefore either disobeys outright or runs in the opposite direction. The secret, therefore, is to teach the dog a game and, when you want him to come to you, simply play the game. It is practically a no-fail solution!

To begin, have several members of your family take a few food treats and each go into a different room in the house. Everyone takes turns calling the dog, and each person should

CONSISTENCY PAYS OFF
Dogs need consistency in their feeding schedule, exercise and relief visits, and in the verbal commands you use. If you use "Stay" on Monday and "Stay here, please" on Tuesday, you will confuse your dog. Don't demand perfect behavior during training sessions and then let him have the run of the house the rest of the day. Above all, lavish praise on your pet consistently every time he does something right. The more he feels he is pleasing you, the more willing he will be to learn.

Teaching your Canaan to stay is not too difficult, but it does take patience and perseverance. Trainers usually use a combination of verbal commands and hand signals.

important things to teach a dog, but there are trainers who work with thousands of dogs and never teach the actual word "come." Yet these dogs will race to respond to a person who uses the dog's name followed by "Where are you?" For example, a woman has a elderly companion dog who went blind, but who never fails to locate her owner when asked, "Where are you?"

Children, in particular, love to play this game with their dogs. Children can hide in smaller places like a shower or bath, behind a bed or under a table. The dog needs to work a little bit harder to find these hiding places, but, when he does, he loves to celebrate with a treat and a tussle with a favorite youngster.

"Where are you?" "I'm right here!" Playing a game is a fun way to get your pup's attention and have him running to you in no time.

celebrate the dog's finding him with a treat and lots of happy praise. When a person calls the dog, he is actually inviting the dog to find him and to get a treat as a reward for winning.

A few turns of the "Where are you?" game and the dog will understand that everyone is playing the game and that each person has a big celebration awaiting the dog's success at locating him or her. Once the dog learns to love the game, simply calling out "Where are you?" will bring him running from wherever he is when he hears that all-important question.

The come command is recognized as one of the most

"COME" . . . BACK
Never call your dog to come to you for a correction or scold him when he reaches you. That is the quickest way to turn a come command into "Go away fast!" Dogs think only in the present tense, and your dog will connect the scolding with coming to you, not with the misbehavior of a few moments earlier.

TEACHING HEEL

Heeling means that the dog walks beside the owner without pulling. It takes time and patience on the owner's part to succeed at teaching the dog that he (the owner) will not proceed unless the dog is walking calmly beside him. Neither pulling out ahead on the lead nor lagging behind is acceptable.

Begin by holding the lead in your left hand as the dog sits beside your left leg. Move the loop end of the lead to your right hand, but keep your left hand short on the lead so that it keeps the dog in close next to you.

Say "Heel" and step forward on your left foot. Keep the dog close to you and take three steps. Stop and have the dog sit next to you in what we now call the heel position. Praise verbally, but do not touch the dog. Hesitate a moment and begin again with "Heel," taking three steps and stopping, at which point the dog is told to sit again.

Your goal here is to have the dog walk those three steps without pulling on the lead. Once he will walk calmly beside you for three steps without pulling, increase the number of steps you take to five. When he will walk politely beside you while you take five steps, you can increase the length of your walk to ten steps. Keep increasing the length of your stroll until the dog will walk quietly beside you without pulling as long as you want him to heel. When you stop heeling, indicate to the dog that the exercise is over by verbally praising as you pet him and say "OK, good dog." The "OK" is used as a release word, meaning that the exercise is finished and the dog is free to relax.

If you are dealing with a dog who insists on pulling you around, simply "put on your brakes" and stand your ground until the dog realizes that the two

THE STUDENT'S STRESS TEST

During training sessions, you must be able to recognize signs of stress in your dog such as:
- tucking his tail between his legs
- lowering his head
- shivering or trembling
- standing completely still or running away
- panting and/or salivating
- avoiding eye contact
- flattening his ears back
- urinating submissively
- rolling over and lifting a leg
- grinning or baring teeth
- aggression when restrained

If your four-legged student displays these signs, he may just be nervous or intimidated. The training session may have been too lengthy, with not enough praise and affirmation. Stop for the day and try again tomorrow.

of you are not going anywhere until he is beside you and moving at your pace, not his. It may take some time just standing there to convince the dog that you are the leader and that you will be the one to decide on the direction and speed of your travel.

Each time the dog looks up at you or slows down to give a slack lead between the two of you, quietly praise him and say, "Good heel. Good dog." Eventually, the dog will begin to respond and within a few days he will be walking politely beside you without pulling on the lead. At first, the training sessions should be kept short and very positive; soon the dog will be able to walk nicely with you for increasingly longer distances. Remember also to give the dog free time and the opportunity to run and play when you have finished heel practice.

WEANING OFF FOOD IN TRAINING

Food is used in training new behaviors. Once the dog understands what behavior goes with a specific command, it is time to start weaning him off the food treats. At first, give a treat after each exercise. Then, start to give a treat only after every other exercise. Mix up the times when you offer a food reward and the times when you only offer praise so that the dog will never know when he is going to receive both food and praise and when he is going to receive only praise. This is called a variable ratio reward system. It proves successful because there is always the chance that the owner will produce a treat, so the dog never stops trying for that reward. No matter what, *always* give verbal praise.

OBEDIENCE CLASSES

It is a good idea to enroll in an obedience class if one is available in your area. If yours is a show dog, showing classes would be more appropriate. Many areas have dog clubs that offer basic obedience training as well as preparatory classes for obedience competition. There are also local dog trainers who offer similar classes.

At obedience trials, dogs can earn titles at various levels of competition. The beginning levels of obedience competition include basic behaviors such as sit, down, heel, etc. The more advanced levels of competition include jumping, retrieving, scent discrimination and signal work. The advanced levels require a dog and owner to put a lot of time and effort into their training. The titles that can be earned at these levels of competition are very prestigious.

OTHER ACTIVITIES FOR LIFE

Whether a dog is trained in the structured environment of a class

Although you will decrease the frequency of food rewards as your dog learns, an occasional treat is always a welcome reward for a job well done.

or alone with his owner at home, there are many activities that can bring fun and rewards to both owner and dog once they have mastered basic control.

Teaching the dog to help out around the home, in the garden or on the farm provides great satisfaction to both dog and owner. In addition, the dog's help makes life a little easier for his owner and raises his stature as a valued companion to his family. It helps give the dog a purpose by occupying his mind and providing an outlet for his energy.

Backpacking is an exciting and healthy activity that the dog can be taught without assistance

OBEDIENCE SCHOOL

A basic obedience beginner's class usually lasts for six to eight weeks. Dog and owner attend an hour-long lesson once a week and practice for a few minutes, several times a day, each day at home. If done properly, the whole procedure will result in a well-mannered dog and an owner who delights in living with a pet that is eager to please and enjoys doing things with his owner.

from more than his owner. The exercise of walking and climbing is good for man and dog alike, and the bond that they develop together is priceless. The rule for backpacking with any dog is never to expect the dog to carry more than one-sixth of his body weight.

If you are interested in participating in organized competition with your Canaan, there are activities other than obedience in which you and your dog can become involved. Herding trials and tracking tests are two areas that you should investigate with your breed club. Additionally, agility is a popular sport for all breeds. At these trials, dogs run through obstacle courses that include various jumps, tunnels and other exercises to test the dog's speed and coordination. The owners run beside their dogs to give commands and to guide them through the course. Although competitive, the focus is on fun—it's fun to do, fun to watch and great exercise. Given the versatility and agility of the Canaan Dog, the sky's the limit if you have the patience and dedication to train your dog to succeed.

Facing page: There are wonderful people who enjoy their dogs so much that they make them important parts of their lives. People like this are great assets to the Canaan Dog breed.

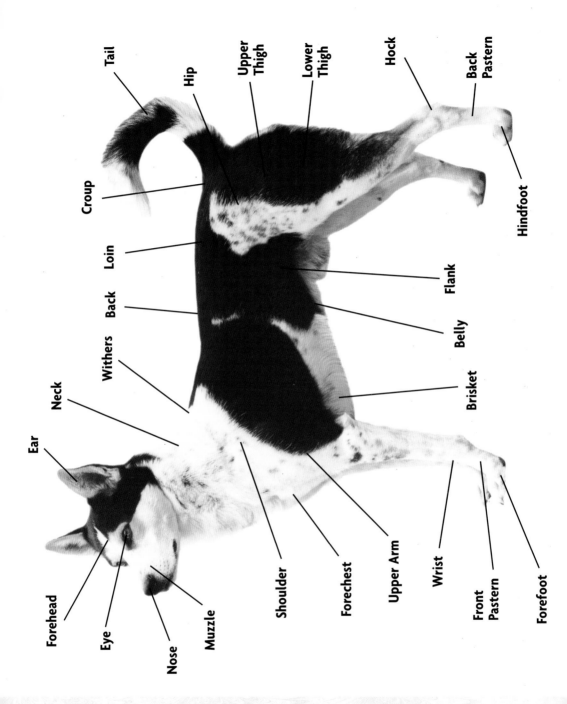

PHYSICAL STRUCTURE OF THE CANAAN DOG

Tail

Croup

Hip

Upper Thigh

Lower Thigh

Hock

Back Pastern

Hindfoot

Loin

Flank

Back

Belly

Withers

Neck

Brisket

Ear

Shoulder

Forechest

Upper Arm

Wrist

Front Pastern

Forefoot

Forehead

Eye

Nose

Muzzle

HEALTH CARE OF YOUR
CANAAN DOG

Dogs suffer from many of the same physical illnesses as people and might even share many of the same psychological problems. Since people usually know more about human diseases than canine maladies, many of the terms used in this chapter will be familiar but not necessarily those used by vets. For example, we will use the familiar term "x-ray" instead of "radiograph." We will also use the familiar term "symptoms," even though dogs don't have symptoms, which are verbal descriptions of something the patient feels or observes himself that he regards as abnormal. Dogs have "clinical signs" since they cannot speak, so we have to look for these clinical signs...but we still use the term "symptoms" in the book.

Medicine is a constantly changing art, with some scientific input as well. Things alter as we learn more and more about basic sciences such as genetics and biochemistry, and have use of more sophisticated imaging techniques like Computer Aided Tomography (CAT scans) or Magnetic Resonance Imaging (MRI scans). There is academic dispute about many canine maladies, so different vets treat them in different ways, and some vets have a greater emphasis on surgical techniques than others.

SELECTING A QUALIFIED VET

Your selection of a vet should be based on personal recommendation for his skills with pets, particularly dogs. If the vet is based nearby, it will be helpful because you might have an emergency or need to make multiple visits for treatments.

All veterinary professionals are licensed and are capable of handling routine medical issues such as infections, injuries and the promotion of health (for example, by vaccination). If the problem affecting your dog is more complex, your vet will refer your pet to someone with a more detailed knowledge of what is wrong. This will usually be a specialist at the nearest university veterinary school who is a veterinary dermatologist, veterinary ophthalmologist, etc; whichever is the relevant field.

Veterinary procedures are very

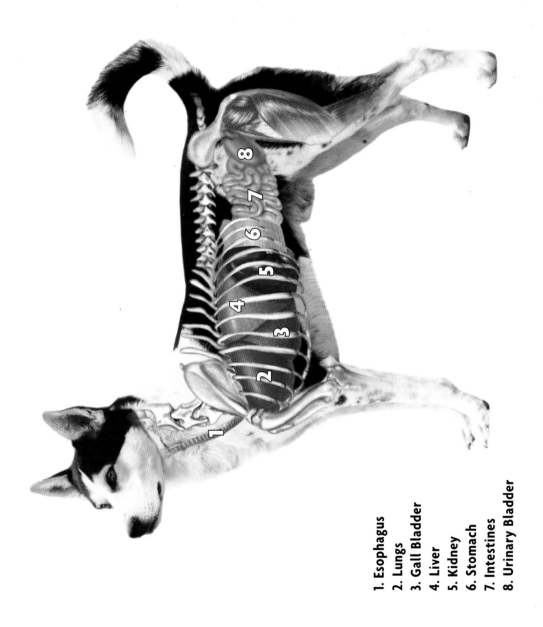

1. Esophagus
2. Lungs
3. Gall Bladder
4. Liver
5. Kidney
6. Stomach
7. Intestines
8. Urinary Bladder

INTERNAL ORGANS OF THE CANAAN DOG

costly and, as the treatments available improve, they are going to become more expensive. It is quite acceptable to discuss matters of cost with your vet; if there is more than one treatment option, cost may be a factor in deciding which route to take.

PREVENTATIVE MEDICINE

It is much easier, less costly and more effective to practice preventative medicine than to fight bouts of illness and disease. Properly bred puppies of all breeds come from parents that were selected based upon their genetic disease profiles. The puppies' mother should have been vaccinated, free of all internal and external parasites and properly nourished. For these reasons, a visit to the vet who cared for the dam (mother) is recommended if at all possible. The dam passes disease resistance to her puppies, which should last from eight to ten weeks. Unfortunately, she can also pass on parasites and infection. This is why knowledge about her health is useful in learning more about the health of the puppies.

WEANING TO FIVE MONTHS OLD

Puppies should be weaned by the time they are two months old. A puppy that remains for at least eight weeks with its mother and littermates usually adapts better to other dogs and people later in its life.

Breakdown of Veterinary Income by Category

2%	Dentistry
4%	Radiology
12%	Surgery
15%	Vaccinations
19%	Laboratory
23%	Examinations
25%	Medicines

A typical vet's income, categorized according to services performed. This survey dealt with small-animal (pets) practices.

Some new owners have their puppy examined by a vet immediately, which is a good idea unless the puppy is overtired by a long journey. Vaccination programs usually begin when the puppy is very young.

The puppy will have its teeth examined and have its skeletal conformation and general health checked prior to certification by the vet. Puppies in certain breeds have problems with their kneecaps, cataracts and other eye problems, heart murmurs and undescended testicles. They may also have personality problems and your vet might have training in temperament testing and evaluation.

VACCINATION SCHEDULING

Most vaccinations are given by injection and should only be given by a vet. Both he and you

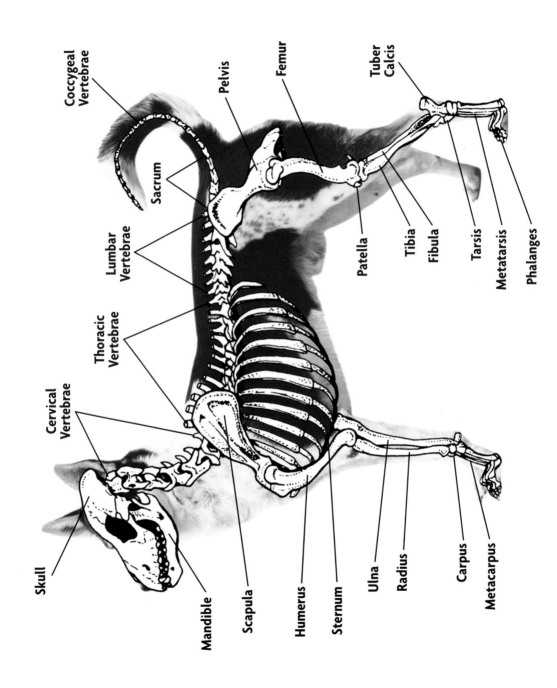

Coccygeal Vertebrae

Pelvis

Femur

Tuber Calcis

Sacrum

Lumbar Vertebrae

Thoracic Vertebrae

Cervical Vertebrae

Patella

Tibia

Fibula

Tarsis

Metatarsis

Phalanges

Skull

Mandible

Scapula

Humerus

Sternum

Ulna

Radius

Carpus

Metacarpus

SKELETAL STRUCTURE OF THE CANAAN DOG

should keep a record of the date of the injection, the identification of the vaccine and the amount given. Some vets give a first vaccination at eight weeks, but most dog breeders prefer the course not to commence until about ten weeks because of the risk of interaction with the antibodies produced by the mother. The vaccination scheduling is usually based on a 15-day cycle. You must take your vet's advice as to when to vaccinate, as this may differ according to the vaccine used.

The usual vaccines contain immunizing doses of several different viruses such as distemper, parvovirus, parainfluenza and hepatitis. There are other vaccines available when the puppy is at risk. You should rely upon professional advice. This is especially true for the booster immunizations. Most vaccination programs require a booster when the puppy is a year old and once a year thereafter. In some cases, circumstances may require more or less frequent immunizations. Discuss parvovirus with your breeder, as this gastrointestinal virus commonly affects Canaan pups.

Kennel cough, more formally known as tracheobronchitis, is immunized against with a vaccine that is sprayed into the dog's nostrils. Kennel cough is usually included in routine vaccination, but it is often not as effective as the vaccines for other major diseases.

FIVE MONTHS TO ONE YEAR OF AGE
Unless you intend to breed or show your dog, neutering the puppy at six months of age is recommended. Discuss this with your vet. Neutering/spaying has proven to be extremely beneficial to male and female puppies, respectively. Besides eliminating the possibility of pregnancy, it inhibits (but does not prevent) breast cancer in bitches and prostate cancer in male dogs. Under no circumstances should a bitch be spayed prior to her first season.

Your vet should provide your puppy with a thorough dental evaluation at six months of age, ascertaining whether all of the permanent teeth have erupted properly. A home dental-care regimen should be initiated at six months, including brushing weekly and providing good dental devices (such as nylon bones). Regular dental care promotes healthy teeth, fresh breath and a longer life.

DOGS OLDER THAN ONE YEAR
Continue to visit the vet at least once a year. There is no such disease as "old age," but bodily functions do change with age. The eyes and ears are no longer as efficient. Liver, kidney and

intestinal functions often decline. Proper dietary changes, recommended by your vet, can make life more pleasant for your aging Canaan Dog and you.

SKIN PROBLEMS

Vets are consulted by dog owners for skin problems more than for any other group of diseases or maladies. A dog's skin is as sensitive, if not more so, than human skin, and both suffer almost the same ailments (though the occurrence of acne in most breeds of dog is rare!). For this reason, veterinary dermatology has developed into a specialty practiced by many veterinary professionals.

Since many skin problems have visual symptoms that are almost identical, it requires the skill of an experienced veterinary dermatologist to identify and cure many of the more severe skin disorders. Pet shops sell many treatments for skin problems, but most of the treatments are directed at symptoms and not at the underlying problem(s). If your dog is suffering from a skin disorder, you should seek professional assistance as quickly as

HEALTH AND VACCINATION SCHEDULE

AGE IN WEEKS:	6TH	8TH	10TH	12TH	14TH	16TH	20-24TH	52ND
Worm Control	✔	✔	✔	✔	✔	✔	✔	
Neutering								✔
Heartworm		✔		✔		✔	✔	
Parvovirus	✔		✔		✔		✔	✔
Distemper		✔		✔		✔		✔
Hepatitis		✔		✔		✔		✔
Leptospirosis								✔
Parainfluenza	✔		✔		✔			✔
Dental Examination		✔					✔	✔
Complete Physical		✔					✔	✔
Coronavirus				✔			✔	✔
Kennel Cough	✔							
Hip Dysplasia								✔
Rabies						✔		

Vaccinations are not instantly effective. It takes about two weeks for the dog's immune system to develop antibodies. Most vaccinations require annual booster shots. Your veterinarian should guide you in this regard.

DISEASE REFERENCE CHART

	What is it?	What causes it?	Symptoms
Leptospirosis	Severe disease that affects the internal organs; can be spread to people.	A bacterium, which is often carried by rodents, that enters through mucous membranes and spreads quickly throughout the body.	Range from fever, vomiting and loss of appetite in less severe cases to shock, irreversible kidney damage and possibly death in most severe cases.
Rabies	Potentially deadly virus that infects warm-blooded mammals.	Bite from a carrier of the virus, mainly wild animals.	1st stage: dog exhibits change in behavior, fear. 2nd stage: dog's behavior becomes more aggressive. 3rd stage: loss of coordination, trouble with bodily functions.
Parvovirus	Highly contagious virus, potentially deadly.	Ingestion of the virus, which is usually spread through the feces of infected dogs.	Most common: severe diarrhea. Also vomiting, fatigue, lack of appetite.
Kennel cough	Contagious respiratory infection.	Combination of types of bacteria and virus. Most common: *Bordetella bronchiseptica* bacteria and parainfluenza virus.	Chronic cough.
Distemper	Disease primarily affecting respiratory and nervous system.	Virus that is related to the human measles virus.	Mild symptoms such as fever, lack of appetite and mucus secretion progress to evidence of brain damage, "hard pad."
Hepatitis	Virus primarily affecting the liver.	Canine adenovirus type I (CAV-1). Enters system when dog breathes in particles.	Lesser symptoms include listlessness, diarrhea, vomiting. More severe symptoms include "blue-eye" (clumps of virus in eye).
Coronavirus	Virus resulting in digestive problems.	Virus is spread through infected dog's feces.	Stomach upset evidenced by lack of appetite, vomiting, diarrhea.

possible. As with all diseases, the earlier a problem is identified and treated, the more likely that the cure will be successful.

HEREDITARY SKIN DISORDERS

Veterinary dermatologists are currently researching a number of skin disorders that are believed to have a hereditary basis. These inherited diseases are transmitted by both parents, who appear (phenotypically) normal but have a recessive gene for the disease, meaning that they carry, but are not affected by, the disease. These diseases pose serious problems to breeders because in some instances there are no methods of identifying carriers. Often the secondary diseases associated with these skin conditions are even more debilitating than the skin disorders themselves, including cancers and respiratory problems.

Among the hereditary skin disorders for which the mode of inheritance is known are acrodermatitis, cutaneous asthenia (Ehlers-Danlos syndrome), sebaceous adenitis, cyclic hematopoiesis, dermatomyositis, IgA deficiency, color dilution alopecia and nodular dermatofibrosis. Some of these disorders are

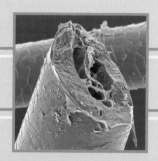

Normal hairs of a dog enlarged 200 times original size. The cuticle (outer covering) is clean and healthy. Unlike human hair that grows from the base, a dog's hair also grows from the end. Damaged hairs and split ends, illustrated above.

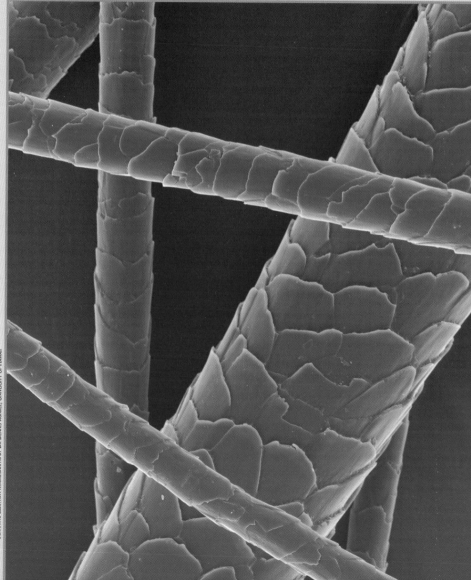

limited to one or two breeds, while others affect a large number of breeds. All inherited diseases must be diagnosed and treated by a veterinary specialist.

PARASITE BITES

Many of us are allergic to insect bites. The bites itch, erupt and may even become infected. Dogs have the same reaction to fleas, ticks and/or mites. When an insect lands on you, you have the chance to whisk it away with your hand. Unfortunately, when a dog is bitten by a flea, tick or mite, it can only scratch it away or bite it. By the time the dog has been bitten, the parasite has done some of its damage. It may also have laid eggs, which will cause problems in the near future. The itching from parasite bites is probably due to the saliva injected into the site when the parasite sucks the dog's blood.

AIRBORNE ALLERGIES

Just as humans suffer from hay fever during the pollinating season, many dogs suffer from the same allergies. When the pollen count is high, your dog might suffer, but don't expect him to sneeze and have a runny nose as a human would. Dogs react to pollen allergies in the same way they react to fleas—they scratch and bite themselves. Dogs, like humans, can be tested for allergens. Discuss the testing with your vet.

AUTO-IMMUNE ILLNESSES

An auto-immune illness is one in which the immune system overacts and does not recognize parts of the affected person; rather, the immune system starts to react as if these parts were foreign and need to be destroyed. An example is rheumatoid arthritis, which occurs when the body does not recognize the joints, thus leading to a very painful and damaging reaction in the joints. This has nothing to do with age, so can occur in children. The wear-and-tear arthritis of the older person or dog is osteo-arthritis.

Lupus is an auto-immune disease that affects dogs as well as people. It can take variable forms, affecting the kidneys, bones and the skin. It can be fatal, so is treated with steroids, which can themselves have very significant side effects. The steroids calm down the allergic reaction to the body's tissues, which helps the lupus, but also decreases the body's reaction to real foreign substances such as bacteria, and also thins the skin and bone.

FOOD PROBLEMS

FOOD ALLERGIES

Dogs are allergic to many foods that are best-sellers and highly recommended by breeders and vets. Changing the brand of food that you buy may not eliminate the problem if the element to which the dog is allergic is contained in the new brand.

Recognizing a food allergy can be difficult. Humans often have rashes when they eat foods to which they are allergic, or have swelling of the lips or eyes. Dogs do not usually develop rashes, but react in the same way as they to an airborne or bite allergy—they itch, scratch and bite. While pollen allergies and parasite bites are usually seasonal, food allergies are year-round problems.

PROPER DIET

Feeding your dog properly is very important. An incorrect diet could affect the dog's health, behavior and nervous system, possibly making a normal dog into an aggressive one. Its most visible effects are to the skin and coat, but internal organs are similarly affected.

TREATING FOOD ALLERGY

Diagnosis of food allergy is based on a two- to four-week dietary trial with a home-cooked diet fed to the exclusion of all other foods. The diet should consist of boiled rice or potato with a source of protein that the dog has never eaten before, such as fresh or frozen fish, lamb or even something as exotic as pheasant. Water has to be the only drink, and it is really important that no other foods are fed during this trial. If the dog's condition improves, you will need to try the original diet once again to see if the itching resumes. If it does, then this confirms the diagnosis that the dog is allergic to its original diet. The treatment is long-term feeding of something that does not distress the dog's skin, which may be in the form of one of the commercially available hypoallergenic diets or the home-made diet that you created for the allergy trial.

FOOD INTOLERANCE

Food intolerance is the inability of the dog to completely digest certain foods. This occurs because the dog does not have the chemicals necessary to digest some foodstuffs. These chemicals are called enzymes. All puppies have the enzymes necessary to digest canine milk, but some dogs do not have the enzymes to digest a very different form of milk that is commonly found in human households—milk from cows. In such dogs, drinking cows' milk results in loose bowels, stomach pains and the passage of gas.

Dogs often do not have the enzymes to digest soy or other beans. The treatment is to exclude the foodstuffs that upset your Canaan's digestion.

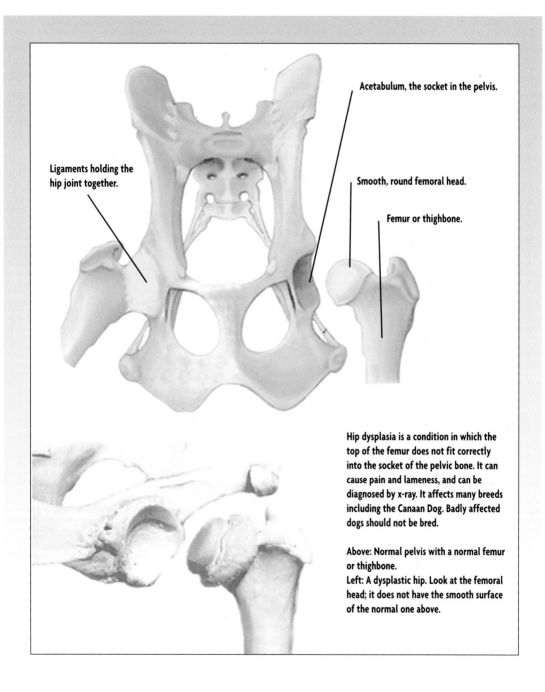

Acetabulum, the socket in the pelvis.

Ligaments holding the hip joint together.

Smooth, round femoral head.

Femur or thighbone.

Hip dysplasia is a condition in which the top of the femur does not fit correctly into the socket of the pelvic bone. It can cause pain and lameness, and can be diagnosed by x-ray. It affects many breeds including the Canaan Dog. Badly affected dogs should not be bred.

Above: Normal pelvis with a normal femur or thighbone.
Left: A dysplastic hip. Look at the femoral head; it does not have the smooth surface of the normal one above.

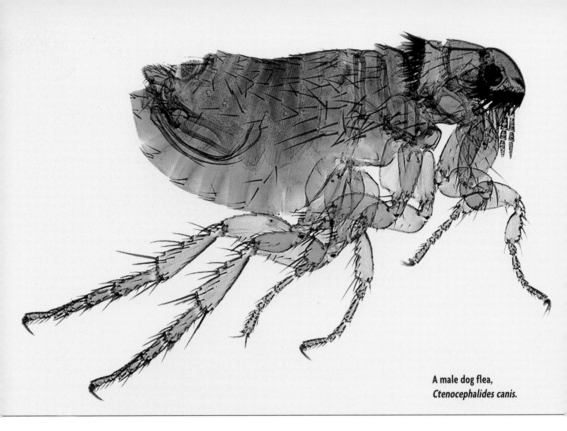

A male dog flea,
Ctenocephalides canis.

EXTERNAL PARASITES

FLEAS

Of all the problems to which dogs are prone, none is more well known and frustrating than fleas. Flea infestation is relatively simple to cure but difficult to prevent. Parasites that are harbored inside the body are a bit more difficult to eradicate but they are easier to control.

To control flea infestation, you have to understand the flea's life cycle. Fleas are often thought of as a summertime problem, but centrally heated homes have changed the patterns and fleas can be found at any time of the year.

The most effective method of flea control is a two-stage approach: one stage to kill the adult fleas, and the other to control the development of pre-adult fleas. Unfortunately, no single active ingredient is effective against all stages of the life cycle.

LIFE CYCLE STAGES

During its life, a flea will pass through four life stages: egg, larva, pupa and adult. The adult stage is the most visible and irritating stage of the flea life cycle, and this is why the majority of flea-control products concentrate on this stage. The fact is that adult fleas account for only 1% of the total flea population, and the other 99% exist in pre-adult stages, i.e. eggs, larvae and pupae. The pre-adult stages are barely visible to the naked eye.

THE LIFE CYCLE OF THE FLEA

Eggs are laid on the dog, usually in quantities of about 20 or 30, several times a day. The adult female flea must have a blood meal before each egg-laying session. When first laid, the eggs will cling to the dog's hair, as the eggs are still moist. However, they will quickly dry out and fall from the dog, especially if the dog moves around or scratches. Many eggs will fall off in the dog's favorite area or an area in which he spends a lot of time, such as his bed.

Once the eggs fall from the dog onto the carpet or furniture, they will hatch into larvae. This takes from one to ten days. Larvae are not particularly mobile and will usually travel only a few

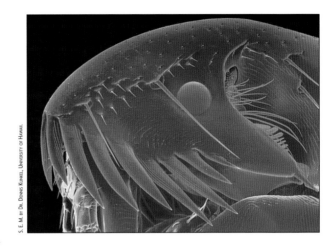

S. E. M. BY DR. DENNIS KUNKEL, UNIVERSITY OF HAWAII.

Magnified head of a dog flea, *Ctenocephalides canis*, colorized for effect.

inches from where they hatch. However, they do have a tendency to move away from bright light and heavy traffic—under furniture and behind doors are common places to find high quantities of flea larvae.

The flea larvae feed on dead organic matter, including adult flea feces, until they are ready to change into adult fleas. Fleas will usually remain as larvae for around seven days. After this period, the larvae will pupate into protective pupae. While inside the pupae, the larvae will undergo metamorphosis and change into adult fleas. This can take as little time as a few days, but the adult fleas can remain inside the pupae waiting to hatch for up to two years. The pupae are signaled to hatch by certain stimuli, such as physical pressure—the pupae's being stepped on, heat from an animal's lying on the pupae or

FLEA-KILLER CAUTION: "POISON"

Flea killers are poisonous. You should not spray these toxic chemicals on areas of a dog's body that he licks, including his genitals and his face. Flea killers taken internally are a better answer, but check with your vet in case internal therapy is not advised for your dog.

The dog flea is the most common parasite found on pet dogs.

S. E. M. by Dr. Dennis Kunkel, University of Hawaii.

increased carbon-dioxide levels and vibrations—indicating that a suitable host is available.

Once hatched, the adult flea must feed within a few days. Once the adult flea finds a host, it will not leave voluntarily. It only becomes dislodged by grooming or the host animal's scratching. The adult flea will remain on the host for the duration of its life unless forcibly removed.

Dwight R Kuhn's magnificent action photo, showing a flea jumping from a dog's back.

TREATING THE ENVIRONMENT AND THE DOG

Treating fleas should be a two-pronged attack. First, the environment needs to be treated; this includes carpets and furniture, especially the dog's bedding and areas underneath furniture. The environment should be treated with a household spray containing an Insect Growth Regulator (IGR) and an insecticide to kill the adult fleas. Most IGRs are effective against eggs and larvae; they actually mimic the fleas' own hormones and stop the eggs and larvae from developing into adult fleas. There are currently no treatments available to attack the pupa stage of the life cycle, so the adult insecticide is used to kill the newly hatched adult fleas before they find a host. Most IGRs are active for many months, while adult insecticides are only active for a few days.

When treating with a household spray, it is a good idea to vacuum before applying the product. This stimulates as many pupae as possible to hatch into adult fleas. The vacuum cleaner should also be treated with an insecticide to prevent the eggs and larvae that have been collected in the vacuum bag from hatching.

The second stage of treatment is to apply an adult insecticide to the dog.

Photo by Dwight R. Kuhn.

EN GARDE: CATCHING FLEAS OFF GUARD!

Consider the following ways to arm yourself against fleas:

- Add a small amount of pennyroyal or eucalyptus oil to your dog's bath. These natural remedies repel fleas.
- Supplement your dog's food with fresh garlic (minced or grated) and an hearty amount of brewer's yeast, both of which ward off fleas.
- Use a flea comb on your dog daily. Submerge fleas in a cup of bleach to kill them quickly.
- Confine the dog to only a few rooms to limit the spread of fleas in the home.
- Vacuum daily...and get all of the crevices! Dispose of the bag every few days until the problem is under control.
- Wash your dog's bedding daily. Cover cushions where your dog sleeps with towels, and wash the towels often.

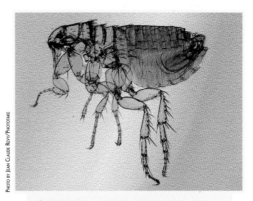

PHOTO BY JEAN CLAUDE REVY/PHOTOTAKE

A LOOK AT FLEAS

Fleas have been around for millions of years and have adapted to changing host animals. They are able to go through a complete life cycle in less than one month or they can extend their lives to almost two years by remaining as pupae or cocoons. They do not need blood or any other food for up to 20 months.

They have been measured as being able to jump 300,000 times and can jump 150 times their length in any direction, including straight up. Those are just a few of the reasons why they are so successful in infesting a dog!

THE LIFE CYCLE OF THE FLEA

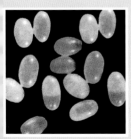

Egg

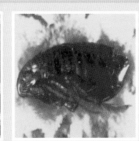

Larva

Pupa

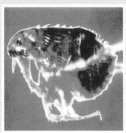

Adult

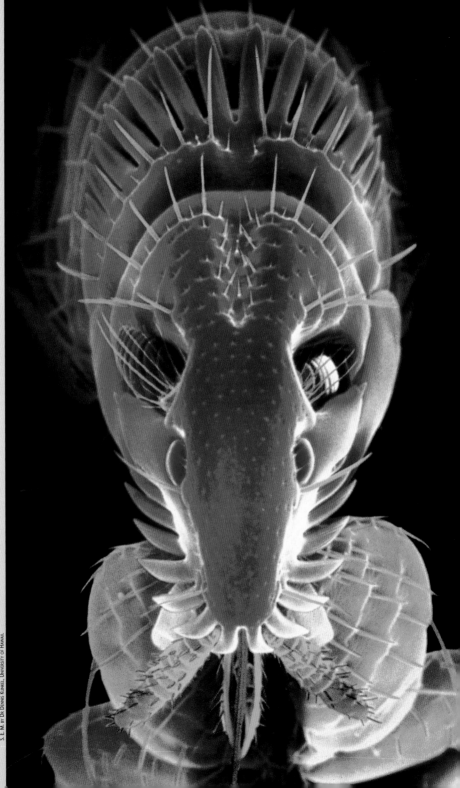

A scanning electron micrograph of a dog or cat flea, *Ctenocephalides,* magnified more than 100x. This image has been colorized for effect.

Traditionally, this would be in the form of a collar or a spray, but more recent innovations include digestible insecticides that poison the fleas when they ingest the dog's blood. Alternatively, there are drops that, when placed on the back of the dog's neck, spread throughout the hair and skin to kill adult fleas.

DO NOT MIX
Never mix flea-control products without first consulting your vet. Some products can become toxic when combined with others and can cause fatal consequences.

INSECT GROWTH REGULATOR (IGR)
Two types of products should be used when treating fleas—a product to treat the pet and a product to treat the home. Adult fleas represent less than 1% of the flea population. The pre-adult fleas (eggs, larvae and pupae) represent more than 99% of the flea population and are found in the environment; it is in the case of pre-adult fleas that products containing an Insect Growth Regulator (IGR) should be used in the home.

IGRs are a new class of compounds used to prevent the development of insects. They do not kill the insect outright, but instead use the insect's biology against it to stop it from completing its growth. Products that contain methoprene are the world's first and leading IGRs. Used to control fleas and other insects, this type of IGR will stop flea larvae from developing and protect the house for up to seven months.

TICKS AND MITES
Though not as common as fleas, ticks and mites are found all over the tropical and temperate world. They don't bite, like fleas; they harpoon. They dig their sharp proboscis (nose) into the dog's skin and drink the blood. Their only food and drink is dog's blood. Dogs can get Lyme disease, Rocky Mountain spotted fever (in the US only), paralysis and many other diseases from ticks and mites. They may live where fleas are found and they like to hide in cracks or seams in walls. They are controlled the same way fleas are controlled.

The dog tick, *Dermacentor variabilis*, may well be the most common dog tick in many geographical areas, especially those areas where the climate is hot and humid. Most dog ticks

A brown dog tick, *Rhipicephalus sanguineus*, is an uncommon but annoying tick found on dogs.

PHOTO BY CAROLINA BIOLOGICAL SUPPLY/PHOTOTAKE.

The head of a dog tick, *Dermacentor variabilis*, enlarged and colorized for effect.

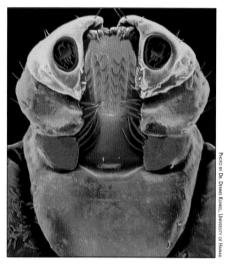

Photo by Dr. Dennis Kunkel, University of Hawaii.

DEER-TICK CROSSING
The great outdoors may be fun for your dog, but it also is an home to dangerous ticks. Deer ticks carry a bacterium known as *Borrelia burgdorferi* and are most active in the autumn and spring. When infections are caught early, penicillin and tetracycline are effective antibiotics, but if left untreated the bacteria may cause neurological, kidney and cardiac problems as well as long-term trouble with walking and painful joints.

have life expectancies of a week to six months, depending upon climatic conditions. They can neither jump nor fly, but they can crawl slowly and can range up to 6 feet to reach a sleeping or unsuspecting dog.

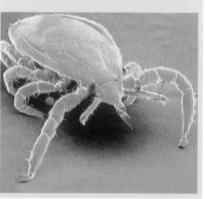

S. E. M. by Dr. Andrew Spielman/Phototake

Human lice look like dog lice; the two are closely related.

Photo by Dwight R. Kuhn.

MANGE

Mites cause a skin irritation called mange. Some mites are contagious, like *Cheyletiella*, ear mites, scabies and chiggers. Mites that infest ears are usually controlled with Lindane,

which can only be administered by a vet, followed by Tresaderm at home. It is essential that your dog be treated for mange as quickly as possible because some forms of mange are transmissible to people.

Opposite page:
The dog tick, *Dermacentor variabilis*, is probably the most common tick found on dogs. Look at the strength in its eight legs! No wonder it's hard to detach them.

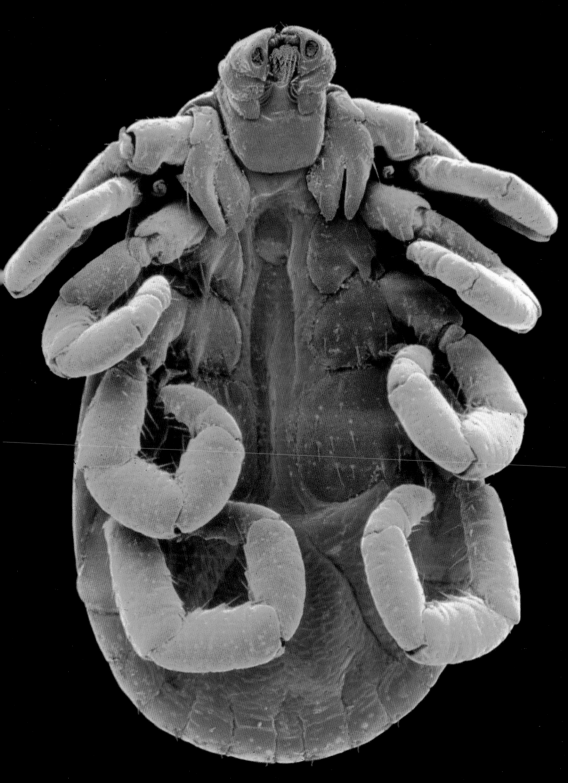

The mange mite,
Psoroptes bovis.

INTERNAL PARASITES

Most animals—fishes, birds and mammals, including dogs and humans—have worms and other parasites that live inside their bodies. According to Dr. Herbert R. Axelrod, the fish pathologist, there are two kinds of parasites: dumb and smart. The smart parasites live in peaceful coopera- tion with their hosts (symbiosis), while the dumb parasites kill their hosts. Most worm infections are relatively easy to control. If they are not controlled, they weaken the host dog to the point that other medical problems occur, but they do not kill the host as dumb parasites would.

ROUNDWORMS

The roundworms that infect dogs are known scientifically as *Toxocara canis*. They live in the dog's intestines and shed eggs continually. It has been estimated that a dog produces about 6 ounces of feces every day. Each ounce of feces averages hundreds of thousands of roundworm eggs. There are no known areas in which dogs roam that do not contain roundworm eggs. The greatest danger of roundworms is

ROUNDWORMS

Average-size dogs can pass 1,360,000 roundworm eggs every day. For example, if there were only 1 million dogs in the world, the world would be saturated with over a thousand tons of dog feces. These feces would contain 15 billion roundworm eggs.

Up to 31% of home yards and children's sand boxes in the US contain roundworm eggs.

Flushing dog's feces down the toilet is not a safe practice because the usual sewage treatments do not destroy roundworm eggs.

Infected puppies start shedding roundworm eggs at three weeks of age. They can be infected by their mother's milk.

PHOTO BY CAROLINA BIOLOGICAL SUPPLY/PHOTOTAKE.

The roundworm *Rhabditis* can infect both dogs and humans.

that they infect people too! It is wise to have your dog tested regularly for roundworms.

Pigs also have roundworm infections that can be passed to humans and dogs. The typical roundworm parasite is called *Ascaris lumbricoides.*

PHOTO BY DWIGHT R. KUHN.

DEWORMING

Ridding your puppy of worms is *very important* because certain worms that puppies carry, such as tapeworms and roundworms, can infect humans.

Breeders initiate deworming programs at or about four weeks of age. The routine is repeated every two or three weeks until the puppy is three months old. The breeder from whom you obtained your puppy should provide you with the complete details of the deworming program.

Your veterinarian can prescribe and monitor the program of deworming for you. The usual program is treating the puppy every 15–20 days until the puppy is positively worm-free. It is advised that you only treat your puppy with drugs that are recommended professionally.

The common roundworm, *Ascaris lumbricoides.*

Left: the hookworm *Ancylostoma caninum.*

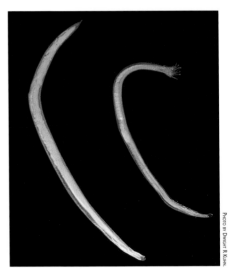

Right: Male and female hookworms.

HOOKWORMS

The worm *Ancylostoma caninum* is commonly called the dog hookworm. It is also dangerous to humans and cats. It has teeth by which it attaches itself to the intestines of the dog. It changes the site of its attachment about six times a day and the dog loses blood from each detachment, possibly causing iron-deficiency anemia. Hookworms are easily purged from the dog with many medications. Milbemycin oxime, which also serves as a heartworm

The infective stage of the hookworm larva.

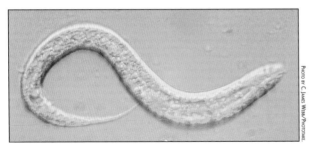

preventative in Collies, can be used for this purpose.

In some regions, the "temperate climate" hookworm (*Uncinaria stenocephala*) is rarely found in pet or show dogs, but can occur in hunting packs, racing Greyhounds and sheepdogs because the worms can be prevalent wherever dogs are exercised regularly on grassland.

TAPEWORMS

There are many species of tapeworm, all of which are carried by fleas! The dog eats the flea and starts the tapeworm cycle. Humans can also be infected with tapeworms—so don't eat fleas! Fleas are so small that your dog could pass them onto your hands, your plate or your food, and thus make it possible for you to ingest a flea that is carrying tapeworm eggs.

TAPEWORMS

Humans, rats, squirrels, foxes, coyotes, wolves and domestic dogs are all susceptible to tapeworm infection. Except in humans, tapeworms are usually not a fatal infection. Infected individuals can harbor 1,000 parasitic worms.

Tapeworms, like some other types of worm, are hermaphroditic, meaning male and female in the same worm.

If dogs eat infected rats or mice, they get the tapeworm disease. One month after attaching to a dog's intestine, the worm starts shedding eggs. These eggs are infective immediately. Infective eggs can live for a few months without a host animal.

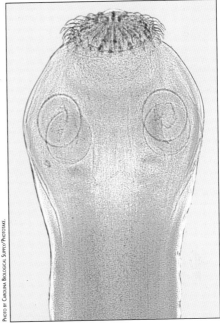

The head and rostellum (the round prominence on the scolex) of a tapeworm, which infects dogs and humans.

PHOTO BY CAROLINA BIOLOGICAL SUPPLY/PHOTOTAKE.

While tapeworm infection is not life-threatening in dogs (smart parasite!), it can be the cause of a very serious liver disease for humans. About 50% of the humans infected with *Echinococcus multilocularis*, a type of tapeworm that causes alveolar hydatis, perish.

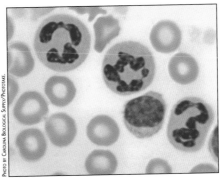

Magnified heartworm larvae, *Dirofilaria immitis.*

PHOTO BY CAROLINA BIOLOGICAL SUPPLY/PHOTOTAKE.

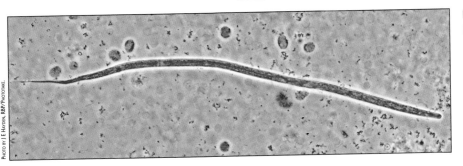

Heartworm, *Dirofilaria immitis.*

PHOTO BY J E HAYDEN, RBP/PHOTOTAKE.

First Aid at a Glance

Burns
Place the affected area under cool water; use ice if only a small area is burnt.

Insect bites
Apply ice to relieve swelling; antihistamine dosed properly.

Animal bites
Clean any bleeding area; apply pressure until bleeding subsides; go to the vet.

Spider bites
Use cold compress and a pressurized pack to inhibit venom's spreading.

Antifreeze poisoning
Induce vomiting with hydrogen peroxide. Seek *immediate* veterinary help!

Fish hooks
Removal best handled by vet; hook must be cut in order to remove.

Snake bites
Pack ice around bite; contact vet quickly; identify snake for proper antivenin.

Car accident
Move dog from roadway with blanket; seek veterinary aid.

Shock
Calm the dog; keep him warm; seek immediate veterinary help.

Nosebleed
Apply cold compress to the nose; apply pressure to any visible abrasion.

Bleeding
Apply pressure above the area; treat wound by applying a cotton pack.

Heat stroke
Submerge dog in cold bath; cool down with fresh air and water; go to the vet.

Frostbite/Hypothermia
Warm the dog with a warm bath, electric blankets or hot water bottles.

Abrasions
Clean the wound and wash out thoroughly with fresh water; apply antiseptic.

 Remember: an injured dog may attempt to bite a helping hand from fear and confusion. Always muzzle the dog before trying to offer assistance.

HEARTWORMS

Heartworms are thin, extended worms up to 12 inches long, which live in a dog's heart and the major blood vessels surrounding it. Dogs may have up to 200 worms. Symptoms may be loss of energy, loss of appetite, coughing, the development of a pot belly and anemia.

Heartworms are transmitted by mosquitoes. The mosquito drinks the blood of an infected dog and takes in larvae with the blood. The larvae, called microfilaria, develop within the body of the mosquito and are passed on to the next dog bitten after the larvae mature. It takes two to three weeks for the larvae to develop to the infective stage within the body of the mosquito. Dogs should be treated at about six weeks of age, and maintained on a prophylactic dose given monthly.

Blood testing for heartworms is not necessarily indicative of how seriously your dog is infected. This is a dangerous disease. Discuss the various preventatives with your vet, as some are not recommended for herding dogs. Together you can choose a safe course of prevention for your Canaan Dog.

The heart of a dog infected with canine heartworm, *Dirofilaria immitis.*

HOMEOPATHY:
an alternative to conventional medicine

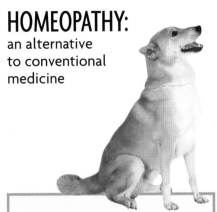

"Less is Most"

Using this principle, the strength of a homeopathic remedy is measured by the number of serial dilutions that were undertaken to create it. The greater the number of serial dilutions, the greater the strength of the homeopathic remedy. The potency of a remedy that has been made by making a dilution of 1 part in 100 parts (or 1/100) is 1c or 1cH. If this remedy is subjected to a series of further dilutions, each one being 1/100, a more dilute and stronger remedy is produced. If the remedy is diluted in this way six times, it is called 6c or 6cH. A dilution of 6c is 1 part in 1,000,000,000,000. In general, higher potencies in more frequent doses are better for acute symptoms and lower potencies in more infrequent doses are more useful for chronic, long-standing problems.

CURING OUR DOGS NATURALLY

Holistic medicine means treating the whole animal as a unique, perfect living being. Generally, holistic treatments do not suppress the symptoms that the body naturally produces, as do most medications prescribed by conventional doctors and vets. Holistic methods seek to cure disease by regaining balance and harmony in the patient's environment. Some of these methods include use of nutritional therapy, herbs, flower essences, aromatherapy, acupuncture, massage, chiropractic and, of course, the most popular holistic approach, homeopathy.

Homeopathy is a theory or system of treating illness with small doses of substances which, if administered in larger quantities, would produce the symptoms that the patient already has. This approach is often described as "like cures like." Although modern veterinary medicine is geared toward the "quick fix," homeopathy relies on the belief that, given the time, the body is able to heal itself and return to its natural healthy state.

Choosing a remedy to cure a problem in our dogs is the difficult part of homeopathy. Consult with your veterinarian for a professional diagnosis of your dog's symptoms. Often these symptoms require immediate conventional care. If your vet is willing, and knowledgeable, you may attempt a homeopathic remedy. Be aware that cortisone prevents homeopathic remedies from working. There are hundreds of possibilities and combinations to cure many problems in dogs, from basic physical problems such as excessive shedding, fleas or other parasites, unattractive doggy odor, bad breath, upset tummy, obesity, dry, oily or dull coat, diarrhea, ear problems or eye discharge (including tears and dry or mucousy matter), to behavioral abnormalities such as fear of loud noises, habitual licking, poor appetite, excessive barking and various phobias. From alumina to zincum metallicum, the remedies span the planet and the imagination…from flowers and weeds to chemicals, insect droppings, diesel smoke and volcanic ash.

Using "Like to Treat Like"

Unlike conventional medicines that suppress symptoms, homeopathic remedies treat illnesses with small doses of substances that, if administered in larger quantities, would produce the symptoms that the patient already has. While the same homeopathic remedy can be used to treat different symptoms in different dogs, here are some interesting remedies and their uses.

Apis Mellifica
(made from honey bee venom) can be used for allergies or to reduce swelling that occurs in acutely infected kidneys.

Diesel Smoke
can be used to help control travel sickness.

Calcarea Fluorica
(made from calcium fluoride, which helps harden bone structure) can be useful in treating hard lumps in tissues.

Natrum Muriaticum
(made from common salt, sodium chloride) is useful in treating thin, thirsty dogs.

Nitricum Acidum
(made from nitric acid) is used for symptoms you would expect to see from contact with acids, such as lesions, especially where the skin joins the linings of body orifices or openings such as the lips and nostrils.

Symphytum
(made from the herb Knitbone, *Symphytum officianale*) is used to encourage bones to heal.

Urtica Urens
(made from the common stinging nettle) is used in treating painful, irritating rashes.

HOMEOPATHIC REMEDIES FOR YOUR DOG

Symptom/Ailment	Possible Remedy
ALLERGIES	Apis Mellifica 30c, Astacus Fluviatilis 6c, Pulsatilla 30c, Urtica Urens 6c
ALOPECIA	Alumina 30c, Lycopodium 30c, Sepia 30c, Thallium 6c
ANAL GLANDS (BLOCKED)	Hepar Sulphuris Calcareum 30c, Sanicula 6c, Silicea 6c
ARTHRITIS	Rhus Toxicodendron 6c, Bryonia Alba 6c
CATARACT	Calcarea Carbonica 6c, Conium Maculatum 6c, Phosphorus 30c, Silicea 30c
CONSTIPATION	Alumina 6c, Carbo Vegetabilis 30c, Graphites 6c, Nitricum Acidum 30c, Silicea 6c
COUGHING	Aconitum Napellus 6c, Belladonna 30c, Hyoscyamus Niger 30c, Phosphorus 30c
DIARRHEA	Arsenicum Album 30c, Aconitum Napellus 6c, Chamomilla 30c, Mercurius Corrosivus 30c
DRY EYE	Zincum Metallicum 30c
EAR PROBLEMS	Aconitum Napellus 30c, Belladonna 30c, Hepar Sulphuris 30c, Tellurium 30c, Psorinum 200c
EYE PROBLEMS	Borax 6c, Aconitum Napellus 30c, Graphites 6c, Staphysagria 6c, Thuja Occidentalis 30c
GLAUCOMA	Aconitum Napellus 30c, Apis Mellifica 6c, Phosphorus 30c
HEAT STROKE	Belladonna 30c, Gelsemium Sempervirens 30c, Sulphur 30c
HICCOUGHS	Cinchona Deficinalis 6c
HIP DYSPLASIA	Colocynthis 6c, Rhus Toxicodendron 6c, Bryonia Alba 6c
INCONTINENCE	Argentum Nitricum 6c, Causticum 30c, Conium Maculatum 30c, Pulsatilla 30c, Sepia 30c
INSECT BITES	Apis Mellifica 30c, Cantharis 30c, Hypericum Perforatum 6c, Urtica Urens 30c
ITCHING	Alumina 30c, Arsenicum Album 30c, Carbo Vegetabilis 30c, Hypericum Perforatum 6c, Mezerium 6c, Sulphur 30c
KENNEL COUGH	Drosera 6c, Ipecacuanha 30c
MASTITIS	Apis Mellifica 30c, Belladonna 30c, Urtica Urens 1m
MOTION SICKNESS	Cocculus 6c, Petroleum 6c
PATELLAR LUXATION	Gelsemium Sempervirens 6c, Rhus Toxicodendron 6c
PENIS PROBLEMS	Aconitum Napellus 30c, Hepar Sulphuris Calcareum 30c, Pulsatilla 30c, Thuja Occidentalis 6c
PUPPY TEETHING	Calcarea Carbonica 6c, Chamomilla 6c, Phytolacca 6c

Recognizing a Sick Dog

Unlike colicky babies and cranky children, our canine charges cannot tell us when they are feeling ill. Therefore, there are a number of signs that owners can identify to know that their dogs are not feeling well.

**Take note for
physical manifestations such as:**

- unusual, bad odor, including bad breath
- excessive shedding
- wax in the ears, chronic ear irritation
- oily, flaky, dull haircoat
- mucus, tearing or similar discharge in the eyes
- fleas or mites
- mucus in stool, diarrhea
- sensitivity to petting or handling
- licking at paws, scratching face, etc.

**Keep an eye out for
behavioral changes as well including:**

- lethargy, idleness
- lack of patience or general irritability
- lack of appetite
- phobias (fear of people, loud noises, etc.)
- strange behavior, suspicion, fear
- coprophagia
- more frequent barking
- whimpering, crying

Get Well Soon

You don't need a DVM or DVR to provide good TLC to your sick or recovering dog, but you do need to pay attention to some details that normally wouldn't bother him. The following tips will aid Fido's recovery and get him back on his paws again:

- Keep his space free of irritating smells, like heavy perfumes and air fresheners.
- Rest is the best medicine! Avoid harsh lighting that will prevent your dog from sleeping. Shade him from bright sunlight during the day and dim the lights in the evening.
- Keep the noise level down. Animals are more sensitive to sound when they are sick.

- Be attentive to any necessary temperature adjustments. A dog with a fever needs a cool room and cold liquids. A bitch that is whelping or recovering from surgery will be more comfortable in a warm room, consuming warm liquids and food.
- You wouldn't send a sick child back to school early, so don't rush your dog back into a full routine until he seems absolutely ready.

Number-One Killer Disease in Dogs: CANCER

In every age, there is a word associated with a disease or plague that causes humans to shudder. In the 21st century, that word is "cancer." Just as cancer is the leading cause of death in humans, it claims nearly half the lives of dogs that die from a natural disease as well as half the dogs that die over the age of ten years.

Described as a genetic disease, cancer becomes a greater risk as the dog ages. Vets and dog owners have become increasingly aware of the threat of cancer to dogs. Statistics reveal that one dog in every five will develop cancer, the most common of which is skin cancer. Many cancers, including prostate, ovarian and breast cancer, can be avoided by spaying and neutering our dogs by the age of six months.

Early detection of cancer can save or extend your dog's life, so it is absolutely vital for owners to have their dogs examined by a qualified vet or oncologist immediately upon detection of any abnormality. Certain dietary guidelines have also proven to reduce the onset and spread of cancer. Foods based on fish rather than beef, due to the presence of Omega-3 fatty acids, are recommended. Other amino acids such as glutamine have significant benefits for canines, particularly those breeds that show a greater susceptibility to cancer.

Cancer management and treatments promise hope for future generations of canines. Since the disease is genetic, breeders should never breed a dog whose parents, grandparents and any related siblings have developed cancer. It is difficult to know whether to exclude an otherwise healthy dog from a breeding program as the disease does not manifest itself until the dog's senior years.

RECOGNIZE CANCER WARNING SIGNS

Since early detection can possibly rescue your dog from becoming a cancer statistic, it is essential for owners to recognize the possible signs and seek the assistance of a qualified professional.

- Abnormal bumps or lumps that continue to grow
- Bleeding or discharge from any body cavity
- Persistent stiffness or lameness
- Recurrent sores or sores that do not heal
- Inappetence
- Breathing difficulties
- Weight loss
- Bad breath or odors
- General malaise and fatigue
- Eating and swallowing problems
- Difficulty urinating and defecating

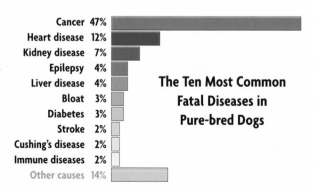

Disease	%
Cancer	47%
Heart disease	12%
Kidney disease	7%
Epilepsy	4%
Liver disease	4%
Bloat	3%
Diabetes	3%
Stroke	2%
Cushing's disease	2%
Immune diseases	2%
Other causes	14%

The Ten Most Common Fatal Diseases in Pure-bred Dogs

A naturally hardy breed, the Canaan Dog enjoys a long lifespan with proper everyday care and regular veterinary checks.

CDS: COGNITIVE DYSFUNCTION SYNDROME
"OLD-DOG SYNDROME"

There are many ways to evaluate "old-dog syndrome." Vets have defined CDS (cognitive dysfunction syndrome) as the gradual deterioration of cognitive abilities. These are indicated by changes in the dog's behavior. When a dog changes his routine response, and maladies have been eliminated as the cause of these behavioral changes, then CDS is the usual diagnosis.

More than half the dogs over eight years old suffer from some form of CDS. The older the dog, the more chance it has of suffering from CDS. In humans, doctors often dismiss the CDS behavioral changes as part of "winding down."

There are four major signs of CDS: frequent potty accidents inside the home, sleeps much more or much less than normal, acts confused, and fails to respond to social stimuli.

SYMPTOMS OF CDS

FREQUENT POTTY ACCIDENTS
- *Urinates in the house.*
- *Defecates in the house.*
- *Doesn't signal that he wants to go out.*

SLEEP PATTERNS
- *Moves much more slowly.*
- *Sleeps more than normal during the day.*
- *Sleeps less during the night.*

CONFUSION
- *Goes outside and just stands there.*
- *Appears confused with a faraway look in his eyes.*
- *Hides more often.*
- *Doesn't recognize friends.*
- *Doesn't come when called.*
- *Walks around listlessly and without a destination.*

FAILURE TO RESPOND TO SOCIAL STIMULI
- *Comes to people less frequently, whether called or not.*
- *Doesn't tolerate petting for more than a short time.*
- *Doesn't come to the door when you return home.*

The term "old" is a qualitative term. For dogs, as well as for their masters, old is relative. Certainly we can all distinguish between a puppy Canaan Dog and an adult Canaan Dog—there are the obvious physical traits, such as size, appearance and facial expressions, and personality traits. Puppies and young dogs like to play with children. Children's natural exuberance is a good match for the seemingly endless energy of young dogs. They like to run, jump, chase and retrieve. When dogs grow older and cease their interaction with children, they are often thought of as being too old to keep pace with the kids. On the other hand, if a Canaan Dog is only exposed to older people or quieter lifestyles, his life will normally be less active and the decrease in his activity level as he ages will not be as obvious.

If people live to be 100 years old, dogs live to be 20 years old. While this might seem like a good rule of thumb, it is very inaccurate. When trying to compare dog years to human years, you cannot make a generalization about all dogs. A long-lived breed, the Canaan Dog commonly lives to be about 14 years of age. Dogs generally are considered physically mature at three years of age (or earlier), but can reproduce even earlier. So generally speaking, the first three years of a dog's life are like seven times that of comparable humans. That means a 3-year-old dog is like a 21-year-old human. However, as the curve of comparison shows, there is no hard and fast rule for comparing dog and human ages. Small breeds tend to live longer than large breeds, some breeds' adolescent periods last longer than others' and some breeds experience rapid periods of growth. The comparison is made even more difficult, for, likewise, not all humans age at the same rate...and human females live longer than human males.

WHAT TO LOOK FOR IN SENIORS

Most vets and behaviorists use the seven-year mark as the time to consider a dog a "senior" or "veteran" though some breeders prefer to wait until the Canaan Dog is eight or nine years of age. Nevertheless, the term "senior" or "veteran" does not imply that the dog is geriatric and has begun to fail in mind and body. Aging is essentially a slowing process. Humans readily admit that they feel a difference in their activity level from age 20 to 30, and then from 30 to 40, etc. By treating the seven-year-old dog as a senior, owners are able to implement certain therapeutic and preventative medical strategies with the help of their vets.

A special-care program should include at least two veterinary visits per year and screening sessions to determine the dog's health status, as well as nutritional counselling. Vets determine the senior dog's health status through a blood smear for a complete blood count, serum chemistry profile with electrolytes, urinalysis, blood pressure check, electrocardiogram, ocular tonometry (pressure on the eyeball) and dental prophylaxis.

Such an extensive program for senior dogs is well advised before owners start to see the obvious physical signs of aging, such as slower and inhibited movement, graying, increased sleep/nap periods and disinterest in play and other activity. This preventative program promises a longer, healthier life for the aging dog.

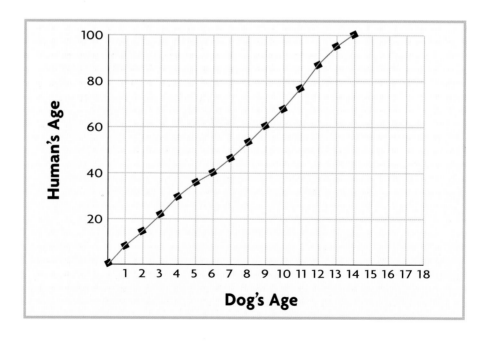

Among the physical problems common in aging dogs are the loss of sight and hearing, arthritis, kidney and liver failure, diabetes mellitus, heart disease and Cushing's disease (a hormonal disease).

In addition to the physical manifestations discussed, there are some behavioral changes and problems related to aging dogs. Dogs suffering from hearing or vision loss, dental discomfort or arthritis can become aggressive. Likewise, the near-deaf and/or blind dog may be startled more easily and react in an unexpectedly aggressive manner. Seniors suffering from senility can become more impatient and irritable. Housesoiling accidents are associated with loss of mobility, kidney problems and loss of sphincter control as well as plaque accumulation, physiological brain changes and reactions to medications. Older dogs, just like young puppies, suffer from separation anxiety, which can lead to excessive barking, whining, housesoiling and destructive behavior. Seniors may become fearful of everyday sounds, such as vacuum cleaners, heaters, thunder and passing traffic. Some dogs have difficulty sleeping, due to discomfort, the need for frequent potty relief and the like.

Owners should avoid spoiling the older dog with too many fatty treats. Obesity is a common problem in older dogs and subtracts years from their lives. Keep the senior dog as trim as possible, since excessive weight puts additional stress on the body's vital organs. Some breeders recommend supplementing the diet with foods high in fiber and lower in calories. Adding fresh vegetables and marrow broth to the senior's diet makes a tasty, low-calorie, low-fat supplement. Vets also offer specialty diets for senior dogs that are worth exploring.

Your dog, as he nears his twilight years, needs your patience and good care more than ever. Never punish an older dog for an accident or abnormal behavior. For all the years of love, protection and companionship that your dog has provided, he deserves special attention and courtesies. The older dog may need to relieve himself at 3 a.m. because he can no longer hold it for eight hours. Older dogs may not be able to remain crated for more than two or three hours. It may be time to give up a sofa or chair to your old friend. Although he may not seem as enthusiastic about your attention and petting, he does appreciate the considerations you offer as he gets older.

Your Canaan Dog does not understand why his world is slowing down. Owners must make their dogs' transition into their golden years as pleasant and rewarding as possible.

WHAT TO DO WHEN THE TIME COMES

You are never fully prepared to make a rational decision about putting your dog to sleep. It is very obvious that you love your Canaan Dog or you would not be reading this book. Putting a beloved dog to sleep is extremely difficult. It is a decision that must be made with your vet. You are usually forced to make the decision when your dog experiences one or more life-threatening symptoms that have become serious enough for you to seek medical (veterinary) help.

If the prognosis of the malady indicates that the end is near and that your beloved pet will only continue to suffer and experience no enjoyment for the balance of its life, then euthanasia is the right choice.

WHAT IS EUTHANASIA?

Euthanasia derives from the Greek, meaning "good death." In other words, it means the planned, painless killing of a dog suffering from a painful, incurable condition, or who is so aged that it cannot walk, see, eat or control its excretory functions. Euthanasia is usually accomplished by injection with an overdose of anesthesia or a barbiturate. Aside from the prick of the needle, the experience is usually painless.

MAKING THE DECISION

The decision to euthanize your dog is never easy. The days during which the dog becomes ill and the end occurs can be unusually stressful for you. If this is your first experience with the death of a loved one, you may need the comfort dictated by your religious beliefs. If you are the head of the family and have children, you should have involved them in the decision of putting your Canaan Dog to sleep. Usually your dog can be maintained on drugs for a few days in order to give you ample time to make a decision. During this time, talking with members of your family or with people who have lived through the same experience can ease the burden of your inevitable decision.

THE FINAL RESTING PLACE

Dogs can have some of the same privileges as humans. The remains of your beloved dog can be buried in a pet cemetery, which is generally expensive. Dogs who have died at home can be buried on your property in a place suitably marked with some stone or newly planted tree or bush, in countries where this is permitted. Alternatively, your dog can be cremated individually and the ashes returned to you. A less expensive option is mass cremation, although, of course, the ashes cannot then be returned. Vets can usually arrange the cremation on your behalf. The cost of these options should always be discussed frankly and openly with your vet.

GETTING ANOTHER DOG?

The grief of losing your beloved dog will be as lasting as the grief of losing a human friend or relative. In most cases, if your dog died of old age (if there is such a thing), it had slowed down considerably. Do you want a new Canaan puppy to replace it? Or are you better off finding a more mature Canaan Dog, say two to three years of age, which will usually be house-trained and will have an already developed personality. In this case, you can find out if you like each other after a few hours of being together.

The decision is, of course, your own. Do you want another Canaan Dog or perhaps a different breed so as to avoid comparison with your beloved friend? Most people usually buy the same breed because they know (and love) the characteristics of that breed. Then, too, they often know people who have the same breed and perhaps they are lucky enough that one of their friends expects a litter soon.

This Canaan bitch, now a senior and still looking alert and healthy, was originally imported from Israel, where she was obtained from nomads.

When you purchase your Canaan Dog, you will make it clear to the breeder whether you want one just as a loveable companion and pet, or if you hope to be buying a Canaan with show prospects. No reputable breeder will sell you a young puppy and tell you that it is *definitely* of show quality, for so much can go wrong during the early months of a puppy's development. If you plan to show, what you will hopefully have acquired is a puppy with "show potential."

To the novice, exhibiting a Canaan in the show ring may look easy, but it takes a lot of hard work and devotion to do top winning at a show such as the prestigious Westminster Kennel Club, Crufts or World Dog Show, not to mention a little luck too!

The first concept that the canine novice learns when watching a dog show is that each dog first competes against members of its own breed. Once the judge has selected the best member of each breed (Best of Breed), provided that the show is judged on a Group system, that chosen dog will compete with

other Best of Breed dogs in its group. Finally, the dogs chosen first in each group will compete for Best in Show.

The second concept that you must understand is that the dogs are not actually compared against one another. The judge compares each dog against its breed standard. While some early breed standards were indeed based on specific dogs that were famous or popular, many dedicated enthusiasts say that a perfect specimen, as described in the standard, has never walked into a show ring, has never been bred and, to the woe of dog breeders around the globe, does not exist. Breeders attempt to get as close to this ideal as possible with every litter, but theoretically the "perfect" dog is so elusive that it is impossible. (And if the "perfect" dog were born, breeders and judges would never agree that it was indeed "perfect.")

If you are interested in exploring the world of dog showing, your best bet is to join your local breed club or the national parent club. These clubs often host both regional and national specialties, shows only for Canaani, which can include conformation as well as obedience and other trials. Even if you have no intention of competing with your Canaan, a specialty is like a festival for lovers of the breed who congregate to share their favorite topic: Canaan Dogs!

Clubs also send out newsletters, and some organize training days and seminars in order that people may learn more about their chosen breed. To locate the breed club closest to you, contact the national kennel club (in the US, the American Kennel Club; in Britain, The Kennel Club), which furnishes the rules and regulations for all of these events plus general dog registration and other basic requirements of dog ownership.

If your Canaan is of age and registered, you can enter him in a dog show where the breed is offered classes. Only unaltered dogs can be entered in a dog show, so if you have spayed or neutered your Canaan, you cannot compete in conformation shows. The reason for this is simple. Dog shows are the main forum to prove which representatives in a breed are worthy of being bred. Only dogs that have achieved championships—the recognized "seal of approval" for quality in pure-bred dogs—should be bred. Altered dogs, however, can participate in other events such as

INTERNATIONAL RECOGNITION

After many years of dedicated work, the Canaan Dog has been heralded with international recognition. In addition to the breed's acceptance in its own national registry, the Israel Kennel Club, the breed is a member of the AKC's Herding Group. Furthermore, the Canaan Dog is recognized by America's United Kennel Club (UKC), where it is exhibited in the Sighthounds and Pariah Dogs Group, and in Canada, where the Canadian Kennel Club (CKC) places it in the Working Group. In Great Britain, the Canaan Dog is granted interim status in the Utility Group (the equivalent of the Non-Sporting Group at AKC events). The FCI recognizes the Canaan Dog in Group 5, Spitz and Primitive Type Dogs. Although all of these kennel clubs seem to designate the breed in different groups, the breed certainly has become a recognizable dog in most major countries of the world.

obedience trials and the Canine Good Citizen program.

Before you actually step into the ring, you would be well advised to sit back and observe the judge's ring procedure. If it is your first time in the ring, do not be over-anxious and run to the front of the line. It is much better to stand back and study how the exhibitor in front of you is performing. The judge asks each handler to "stack" the dog, hopefully showing the dog off to his best advantage. The judge will observe the dog from a distance

Conformation judging is a "hands-on" procedure, as the judge examines the dog's entire body, including his mouth, to check for correct structure. The dog must tolerate this handling and behave politely.

and from different angles, and approach the dog to check his teeth, overall structure, alertness and muscle tone, as well as consider how well the dog "conforms" to the standard. Most importantly, the judge will have the exhibitor move the dog around the ring in some pattern that he should specify (another advantage to not going first, but always listen since some judges change their directions—and the judge is always right!). Finally, the judge will give the dog one last look before moving on to the next exhibitor.

If you are not in the top four in your class at your first show, do not be discouraged. Be patient and consistent, and you may eventually find yourself in a winning line-up. Remember that the winners were once in your shoes and have devoted many hours and much money to earn the placement. If you find that your dog is losing every time and never getting a nod, it may be time to consider a different dog sport or to just enjoy your Canaan as a pet. Parent clubs offer other events, such as agility, tracking, obedience, instinct tests and more, which may be of interest to the owner of a well-trained Canaan.

OBEDIENCE TRIALS
Obedience trials in the US trace back to the early 1930s when

The Canaan Dog Club of America has established a Versatility Program to promote the breed's excellence in the fields of conformation showing, obedience, tracking, herding and agility. Such programs have been very successful in some Sporting and Working Dog breeds, and the unique Canaan Dog benefits greatly from the breeders' efforts in this regard. Dogs must excel in three of the five categories in order to earn the Versatility Award. Canaan Dogs also must pass a hip dysplasia test through the Orthopedic Foundation for Animals (OFA), rating "fair" or better (unless the dog is neutered or spayed).

organized obedience training was developed to demonstrate how well dog and owner could work together. The pioneer of obedience trials is Mrs. Helen Whitehouse Walker, a Standard Poodle fancier, who designed a series of exercises after the Associated Sheep, Police Army Dog Society of Great Britain. Since the days of Mrs. Walker, obedience trials have grown by leaps and bounds, and today there are over 2,000 trials held in the US every year, with more than 100,000 dogs competing. Any registered AKC dog can enter an obedience trial, regardless of conformational disqualifications or neutering.

Obedience trials are divided into three levels of progressive difficulty. At the first level, the Novice, dogs compete for the title Companion Dog (CD); at the intermediate level, the Open, dogs compete for the title Companion Dog Excellent (CDX); and at the advanced level, dogs compete for the title Utility Dog (UD). Classes are sub-divided into "A" (for beginners) and "B" (for more experienced handlers). A perfect score at any level is 200, and a dog must score 170 or better to earn a "leg," of which three are needed to earn the title. To earn points, the dog must score more than 50% of the available points in each exercise; the possible points range from 20 to 40.

Each level consists of a different set of exercises. In the Novice level, the dog must heel on and off lead, come, long sit, long down and stand for examination. These skills are the basic ones required for a well-behaved "Companion Dog." The Open level requires that the dog perform the same exercises above but without a leash for extended lengths of time, as well as retrieve a dumbbell, broad jump and drop on recall. In the Utility level, dogs must perform ten difficult exercises, including scent discrimination, hand signals for basic commands, directed jump and directed retrieve.

Once a dog has earned the UD

title, he can compete with other proven obedience dogs for the coveted title of Utility Dog Excellent (UDX), which requires that the dog win "legs" in ten shows. Utility Dogs who earn "legs" in Open B and Utility B earn points toward their Obedience Trial Champion title. In 1977, the title Obedience Trial Champion (OTCh.) was established by the AKC. To become an OTCh., a dog needs to earn 100 points, which requires three first places in Open B and Utility under three different judges.

AGILITY TRIALS

Having had its origins in the UK back in 1977, AKC agility had its official beginning in the US in August 1994, when the first licensed agility trials were held. The AKC allows all registered breeds (including Miscellaneous Class breeds) to participate, providing the dog is 12 months of age or older. Agility is designed so that the handler demonstrates how well the dog can work at his side. The handler directs his dog over an obstacle course that includes jumps, as well as tires, the dog walk, weave poles, pipe tunnels, collapsed tunnels, etc. While working his way through the course, the dog must keep one eye and ear on the handler and the rest of his body on the course. The handler gives verbal and hand signals to guide the dog through the course.

The first organization to promote agility trials in the US was the United States Dog Agility Association, Inc. (USDAA), which was established in 1986 and spawned numerous member clubs around the country. Both the USDAA and the AKC offer titles to winning dogs. Three titles are available through the USDAA: Agility Dog (AD), Advanced Agility Dog (AAD) and Master Agility Dog (MAD). The AKC offers Novice Agility (NA), Open Agility (OA), Agility Excellent (AX) and Master Agility Excellent (MX). Beyond these four AKC titles, dogs can win additional ones in "jumper" classes, Jumpers with Weave Novice (NAJ), Open (OAJ) and Excellent (MXJ), which lead to the ultimate title(s): MACH, Master Agility Champion. Dogs can continue to add number designations to the MACH titles, indicating how many times the dog has met the MACH requirements, such as MACH1, MACH2, and so on.

Agility is great fun for dog and owner, with many rewards for everyone involved. Interested owners should join a training club that has obstacles and experienced agility handlers who can introduce you and your dog to the "ropes" (and tires, tunnels, jumps, etc.).

TRACKING

Any dog is capable of tracking, using its nose to follow a trail. Tracking tests are exciting and competitive ways to test your Canaan's ability to search and rescue. The AKC started tracking tests in 1937, when the first AKC-licensed test took place as a part of the Utility level at an obedience trial. Ten years later in 1947, the AKC offered the first title, Tracking Dog (TD). It was not until 1980 that the AKC added the Tracking Dog Excellent title (TDX), which was followed by the Versatile Surface Tracking title (VST) in 1995. The title Champion Tracker (CT) is awarded to a dog who has earned all three titles.

In the beginning level of tracking, the owner follows the dog through a field on a long lead. To earn the TD title, the dog must follow a track laid by a human 30 to 120 minutes prior. The track is about 500 yards with up to five directional changes. The TDX requires that the dog follow a track that is three to five hours old over a course up to 1,000 yards with up to seven directional changes. The VST requires that the dog follow a track up to five hours old through an urban setting.

HERDING TRIALS

Herding trials, similar to the sheepdog trials that began in Wales in the late 19th century, have become popular in the US, the UK and beyond. Like dog shows, which were designed to see which owner had the "best dog," herding trials evolved as farmers attempted to determine who had the "best working sheepdog."

The Canaan Dog can participate in herding trials along with fellow herding dogs, even though the breed is not strictly designated as a "Herding" or "Pastoral" breed in every country. These trials are based on the principles of sheep farming, where the dogs must perform a series of tasks against the clock. Moving sheep, gating and separating them and singling out a branded or marked animal are just some of the events in the trial. In the US, the AKC offers herding titles to dogs that excel in these competitions. Among the titles are: Herding Tested (HT), Pre-Trial Tested (PT), Herding Started (HS), Herding Intermediate (HI) and Herding Excellent (HX).

HERDING TRIALS

The first herding trial for Canaan Dogs in America was held in conjunction with the national specialty in 1997. Joan Capiau is the owner of the first Canaan bitch in the world to compete in an all-breed herding trial. Abbey won the High in Trial award at her first event.

FÉDÉRATION CYNOLOGIQUE INTERNATIONALE

Established in 1911, the Fédération Cynologique Internationale (FCI) represents the "world kennel club." This international body brings uniformity to the breeding, judging and showing of pure-bred dogs. Although the FCI originally included only five European nations: France, Germany, Austria, the Netherlands and Belgium (which remains its headquarters), the organization today embraces nations on six continents and recognizes well over 300 breeds of pure-bred dog.

The FCI sponsors both national and international shows. The hosting country determines the judging system and breed standards are always based on the breed's country of origin. Dogs from every country can participate in these impressive canine spectacles, the largest of which is the World Dog Show, hosted in a different country each year.

There are three titles attainable through the FCI: the International Champion, which is the most prestigious; the International Beauty Champion, which is based on aptitude certificates in different countries; and the International Trial Champion, which is based on achievement in obedience trials in different countries. An FCI title requires a dog to win three CACs (*Certificats d'Aptitude au Championnat*), at regional or club shows under three different judges who are breed specialists. The title of International Champion is gained by winning four CACIBs (*Certificats d'Aptitude au Championnat International de Beauté*), which are offered only at international shows, with at least a one-year lapse between the first and fourth award.

The FCI is divided into ten groups. At the World Dog Show, the following classes are offered for each breed: Puppy Class (6–9 months), Junior Class (9–18 months), Open Class (15 months or older) and Champion Class. A dog can be awarded a classification of Excellent, Very Good, Good, Sufficient and Not Sufficient. Puppies can be awarded classifications of Very Promising, Promising or Not Promising. Four placements are made in each class. After all classes are judged, a Best of Breed is selected. Other special groups and classes may also be shown. Each exhibitor showing a dog receives a written evaluation from the judge.

Besides the World Dog Show and other all-breed shows, you can exhibit your dog at specialty shows held by different breed clubs. Specialty shows may have their own regulations.

No matter where in the world the Canaan Dog is shown, the exphasis is on the fact that this is a natural breed. No modifica-tions should be made nor true breed characteris-tics lost in show-ring specimens.

BEHAVIOR OF YOUR
CANAAN DOG

As a Canaan Dog owner, you have selected your dog so that you and your loved ones can have a companion, a protector, a friend and a four-legged family member. You invest time, money and effort to care for and train the family's new charge. Of course, this chosen canine behaves perfectly! Well, perfectly like a *dog*.

THINK LIKE A DOG

Dogs do not think like humans, nor do humans think like dogs, though we try. Unfortunately, a dog is incapable of comprehending how humans think, so the responsibility falls on the owner to adopt a proper canine mindset. Dogs cannot rationalize, and dogs exist in the present moment. Many a dog owner makes the mistake in training of thinking that he can reprimand his dog for something the dog did a while ago. Basically, you cannot even reprimand a dog for something he did 20 seconds ago! Either catch him in the act or forget it! It is a waste of your and your dog's time—in his mind, you are reprimanding him for whatever he is doing at that moment.

The following behavioral problems represent some which owners most commonly encounter. Every dog is unique and every situation is unique. No author could purport for you to solve your Canaan's problems simply by reading a script. Here we outline some basic "dogspeak" so that owners' chances of solving behavioral problems are increased.

Discuss bad habits with your vet and he can recommend a behavioral specialist to consult in appropriate cases. Since behavioral abnormalities are the main reason for owners' abandoning their pets, we hope that you will make a valiant effort to solve your Canaan's problems. Patience and understanding are virtues that must dwell in every pet-loving household.

AGGRESSION

Aggression can be a very big problem in dogs, and, when not controlled, always becomes dangerous. Since Canaani prefer life as "the only dog," they can be somewhat dog-aggressive and require an owner who is aware of the breed's potential for aggressive behavior. An aggressive dog may lunge at, bite or even attack a person or another dog. Aggressive behavior is not to be tolerated. It is more than just inappropriate behavior; it is painful for a family to watch their dog become unpredictable in his behavior to the point where they are afraid of him. While not all aggressive behaviors are dangerous, behaviors like growling, baring teeth, etc., can be frightening. It is important to ascertain why the dog is acting in this manner. Aggression is a display of dominance, and the dog should not have the dominant role in its pack, which is, in this case, your family.

It is important not to challenge an aggressive dog, as this could provoke an attack. Observe your Canaan's body language. Does he make direct eye contact and stare? Does he try to make himself as large as possible: ears pricked, chest out, tail erect? Height and size signify authority

DOMINANT AGGRESSION

Never allow your puppy to growl at you or bare his tiny teeth. Such behavior is dominant and aggressive. If not corrected, the dog will repeat the behavior, which will become more threatening as he grows larger and will eventually lead to biting.

in a dog pack—being taller or "above" another dog literally means that he is "above" in social status. These body signals tell you that your Canaan thinks he is in charge, a problem that needs to be addressed. An aggressive dog is unpredictable; you never know when he is going to strike and what he is going to do. You cannot understand why a dog that is playful one minute is growling the next.

Fear is a common cause of aggression in dogs. Perhaps your Canaan had a negative experience as a puppy, which causes him to be fearful when a similar situation presents itself later in life. The dog may act aggressively in order to protect himself from whatever is making him afraid. It is not always easy to determine what is making your dog fearful, but if you can isolate what brings out the fear reaction, you can help the dog get over it.

Supervise your Canaan's interactions with people and other dogs, and praise the dog when it goes well. If he starts to act aggressively in a situation, correct him and remove him from the situation. Do not let people approach the dog and start petting him without your express permission. That way, you can have the dog sit to accept petting, and praise him when he behaves properly. You are focusing on praise and on modifying his

Although Canaani have "top dog" mentality, they can be socialized to live harmoniously with other dogs. These playmates enjoy some fun time with their owner.

to have as a family pet. If, very unusually, you find that your pet has become untrustworthy and you feel it necessary to seek a new home with a more suitable family and environment, explain fully to the new owners all your reasons for rehoming the dog to be fair to all concerned. In the *very* worst case, you will have to consider euthanasia.

AGGRESSION TOWARD OTHER DOGS

A dog's aggressive behavior toward another dog stems from not enough exposure to other dogs at an early age. If other dogs make your Canaan nervous and agitated, he will lash out as a protective mechanism. A dog that has not received sufficient exposure to other canines tends to think that he is the only dog on the planet. The animal becomes so dominant that he does not even show signs that he is fearful or threatened. Without growling or any other physical signal as a warning, he will lunge at and bite the other dog.

behavior by rewarding him when he acts appropriately. By being gentle and by supervising his interactions, you are showing him that there is no need to be afraid or defensive.

The best solution is to consult a behavioral specialist, one who has experience with the Canaan Dog if possible. Together, perhaps you can pinpoint the cause of your dog's aggression and do something about it. An aggressive dog cannot be trusted, and a dog that cannot be trusted is not safe

A way to correct this is to let your Canaan approach another dog when walking on lead. Watch very closely and, at the first sign of aggression, correct your Canaan and pull him away. Scold him for any sign of discomfort, and then praise him when he ignores the other dog. Keep this up until either he stops the aggressive behavior, learns to ignore other dogs or even accepts other dogs. Praise him lavishly for this correct behavior.

DOMINANT AGGRESSION

A social hierarchy is firmly established in a wild dog pack. The dog wants to dominate those under him and please those above him. Dogs know that there must be a leader, and your Canaan will crown himself emperor if given the chance.

These conflicting innate desires are what a dog owner is up against when he sets about training a dog. In training a dog to obey commands, the owner is reinforcing that he is the "top dog" in the pack and that the dog should, and should want to, serve his superior. Thus, the owner is suppressing the dog's urge to dominate by modifying his behavior and making him obedient.

An important part of training is taking every opportunity to reinforce that you are the leader. The simple action of making your Canaan sit to wait for his food instead of allowing him to run up to get it when he wants it says that you control when he eats; he is dependent on you for food. Although it may be difficult, do not give in to your dog's wishes every time he whines at you or looks at you with pleading eyes. It is a constant effort to show the dog that his place in the pack is at the bottom. This is not meant to sound cruel or inhumane. You love your Canaan and you should treat him with care and affection. You (hopefully) did not get a dog just so you could control another creature. Dog training is not about being cruel or feeling important, it is about molding the dog's behavior into what is acceptable and teaching him to live by your rules. In theory, it is quite simple: catch him in appropriate behavior and reward him for it. Add a dog into the equation and it becomes a bit more trying, but as a rule of thumb, positive reinforcement is what works best.

With a dominant dog, punishment and negative reinforcement can have the opposite effect of what you are after. It can make a

FEAR IN A GROWN DOG

Fear in a grown dog is often the result of improper or incomplete socialization as a pup, or it can be the result of a traumatic experience he suffered when young. Keep in mind that the term "traumatic" is relative—something that you would not think twice about can leave a lasting negative impression on a puppy. If the dog experiences a similar experience later in life, he may try to fight back to protect himself. Again, this behavior is very unpredictable, especially if you do not know what is triggering his fear.

dog fearful and/or act out aggressively if he feels he is being challenged. Remember, a dominant dog perceives himself at the top of the social heap, and will fight to defend his perceived status. The best way to prevent that is to never give him reason to think that he is in control in the first place.

If you are having trouble training your Canaan and it seems as if he is constantly challenging your authority, seek the help of an obedience trainer or behavioral specialist. A professional will work with both you and your dog to teach you effective techniques to use at home. Beware of trainers who rely on excessively harsh methods; scolding is necessary now and then, but the focus in your training should always be on positive reinforcement.

DIGGING

Digging, which is seen as a destructive behavior to humans, is actually quite a natural behavior in dogs. Although terriers (the "earth dogs") are most associated with the digging, any dog's desire to dig can be irrepressible and most frustrating to his owners. Canaani can develop a destructive digging habit if left for hours on end without a job to do. Though Canaani are known as expert escape artists, boredom is usually to blame, as opposed to the need to escape or the pursuit of vermin. The dog feels useful when he digs

and likes to bury things. Thus, when digging occurs in your lawn, it is actually a normal behavior redirected into something the dog can do in his everyday life. In the wild, a dog would be actively seeking food, making his own shelter, etc. He would be using his paws in a purposeful manner for his survival. Since you provide him with food and shelter, he has no need to use his paws for these purposes, and so the energy that he would be using may manifest itself in the form of little holes all over your garden and flower beds.

To eliminate boredom digging, provide the dog with adequate

BE NOT AFRAID
Just like humans, dogs can suffer from phobias including fear of thunder, fear of heights, fear of stairs or even fear of specific objects such as the swimming pool. To help your dog get over his fear, first determine what is causing the phobia. For example, your dog may be generalizing by associating an accident that occurred on one set of stairs with every step he sees. You can try desensitization training, which involves introducing the fear-trigger to your dog slowly, in a relaxed setting, and rewarding him when he remains calm. Most importantly, when your dog responds fearfully, do not coddle or try to soothe him, as this only makes him think that his fear is okay.

HE'S PROTECTING YOU

Barking is your dog's way of protecting you. If he barks at a stranger walking past your house, a moving car or a fleeing cat, he is merely exercising his responsibility to protect his pack (YOU) and territory from a perceived intruder. Since the "intruder" usually keeps going, the dog thinks his barking chased it away and he feels fulfilled. This behavior leads your overly vocal friend to believe that he is the "dog in charge."

BARKING

All Canaani bark, some more so than others. Alert and attentive, especially when outdoors, the Canaan Dog will bark when something or someone enters his environment or when he senses something unusual is occurring. Puppies and adolescents tend to be more vocal than adults, so owners must determine when the Canaan's barking is desired and purposeful, and when it is just showing off and noisy. Barking must be silenced early on before the Canaan develops into a problem barker.

Excessive habitual barking, however, is a problem that should be corrected early on. As your Canaan grows up, you will be able to tell when his barking is purposeful and when it is for

play and exercise so that his mind and paws are occupied, and so that he feels as if he is doing something useful. Digging is easiest to control if it is stopped as soon as possible, but it is often hard to catch a dog in the act. If your dog is a compulsive digger and is not easily distracted by other activities, you can designate an area on your property where he is allowed to dig. If you catch him digging in an off-limits area of the yard, immediately bring him to the approved area and praise him for digging there. Keep a close eye on him so that you can catch him in the act— that is the only way to make him understand what is permitted and what is not. If you take him to a hole he dug an hour ago and tell him "No," he will understand that you are not fond of holes, or dirt or flowers. If you catch him while he is stifle-deep in your tulips, that is when he will get your message.

"Woof!" The Canaan is alert and can be vocal...what is your dog trying to tell you?

no reason. You will become able to distinguish between your dog's different barks and their meanings. For example, the bark when someone comes to the door will be different from the bark when he is excited to see you. It is similar to a person's tone of voice, except that the dog has to rely totally on tone of voice because he does not have the benefit of using words. An incessant barker will be evident at an early age.

There are some things that encourage a dog to bark. For example, if your dog barks non-stop for a few minutes and you give him a treat to quiet him, he believes that you are rewarding him for barking. He will associate barking with getting a treat, and will keep doing it until he is rewarded. On the other hand, if you give him a command such as "Quiet" and praise him after he has stopped barking for a few seconds, he will get the idea that being "quiet" is what you want him to do.

SEXUAL BEHAVIOR

Dogs exhibit certain sexual behaviors that may have influenced your choice of male or female when you first purchased your Canaan. To a certain extent, spaying/neutering will eliminate these behaviors, but if you are purchasing a dog that you wish to breed from, you should be aware

BARKING STANCE
Did you know that a dog is less likely to bark when sitting than standing? Watch your dog the next time that you suspect he is about to start barking. You'll notice that as he does, he gets up on all four feet. Hence, when teaching a dog to stop barking, it helps to get him to sit before you command him to be quiet.

of what you will have to deal with throughout the dog's life.

Female dogs usually have two estruses per year, with each season lasting about three weeks. These are the only times in which a female dog will mate, and she usually will not allow this until the second week of the cycle, although this varies from bitch to bitch. If not bred during the heat cycle, it is not uncommon for a bitch to experience a false pregnancy, in which her mammary glands swell and she exhibits maternal tendencies toward toys or other objects.

With male dogs, owners must be aware that whole dogs (dogs who are not neutered) have the natural inclination to mark their territory. Males mark their territory by spraying small amounts of urine as they lift their legs in a macho ritual. Marking can occur both outdoors in the garden and around the neighborhood as well as indoors on furniture legs, curtains and the sofa. Such behavior can be very frustrating for the owner; early training is strongly urged before the "urge" strikes your dog. Neutering the male at an appropriate early age can solve this problem before it becomes a habit.

Other problems associated with males are wandering and mounting. Both of these habits, of course, belong to the unneutered dog, whose sexual drive leads him away from home in search of the bitch in heat. Males will mount

THE MIGHTY MALE

Males, whether castrated or not, will mount almost anything: a pillow, your leg or, much to your dismay, even your neighbor's leg. As with other types of inappropriate behavior, the dog must be corrected while in the act, which for once is not difficult. Often he will not let go! While a puppy is experimenting with his very first urges, his owners feel he needs to "sow his oats" and allow the pup to mount. As the pup grows into a full-size dog, with full-size urges, it becomes a nuisance and an embarrassment. Males always appear as if they are trying to "save the race," more determined and stronger than imaginable. While altering the dog at an appropriate age will limit the dog's desire, it usually does not remove it entirely.

females in heat, as well as any other dog, male or female, that happens to catch their fancy. Other possible mounting partners include his owner, the furniture, guests to the home and friends you meet on the street. Discourage such behavior early on.

Owners must further recognize that mounting is not merely a sexual expression but also one of dominance, seen in males and females alike. Be consistent and be persistent, and you will find that you can "move mounters."

SEPARATION ANXIETY

Recognized by behaviorists as the most common form of stress for dogs, separation anxiety can also lead to destructive behaviors in your dog. It's more than your Canaan's howling his displeasure at your leaving the house and his being left alone. This is a normal reaction, no different from the child who cries as his mother leaves him on the first day at school. Separation anxiety is more serious. In fact, if you are constantly with your dog, he will come to expect you with him all of the time, making it even more traumatic for him when you are not there.

Obviously, you enjoy spending time with your dog, and he thrives on your love and attention. However, it should not become a dependent relationship in which he is heartbroken without you. This broken heart can also bring on destructive behavior as well as loss of appetite, depression and lack of interest in play and interaction. Canine behaviorists have been spending much time and energy to help owners better understand the significance of this stressful condition.

One thing you can do to minimize separation anxiety is to make your entrances and exits as low-key as possible. Do not give your dog a long drawn-out goodbye, and do not lavish him with hugs and kisses when you return. This is giving in to the attention that he craves, and it will only make him miss it more when you are away. Another thing you can try is to give your dog a treat when you leave; this will not only keep him occupied and keep his mind off the fact that you have just left, but it will also help him associate your leaving with a pleasant experience.

You may have to accustom your dog to being left alone at intervals. Of course, when your dog starts whimpering as you approach the door, your first instinct will be to run to him and comfort him, but do not do it! Really—eventually he will adjust to your absence. His anxiety stems from being placed in an unfamiliar situation; by familiarizing him with being alone, he will learn that he will survive. That is not to say you should purposely leave your dog home

PHARMACEUTICAL FIX

There are two drugs specifically designed to treat mental problems in dogs. About 7 million dogs each year are destroyed because owners can no longer tolerate their dogs' behavior, according to Nicholas Dodman, a specialist in animal behavior at Tufts University in Massachusetts.

The first drug, Clomicalm, is prescribed for dogs suffering from separation anxiety, which is said to cause them to react when left alone by barking, chewing their owners' belongings, drooling copiously or defecating or urinating inside the home.

The second drug, Anipryl, is recommended for cognitive dysfunction syndrome or "old dog syndrome," a mental deterioration that comes with age. Such dogs often seem to forget that they were house-trained and where their food bowls are, and they may even fail to recognize their owners.

A tremendous human-animal bonding relationship is established with all dogs, particularly senior dogs. This precious relationship deteriorates when the dog does not recognize his master. The drug can restore the bond and make senior dogs feel more like their "old selves."

"Let me in!" Dogs of any breed, even independent dogs like Canaani, need the companion-ship of their human families and can suffer from separation anxiety.

As a Canaan Dog owner, you surely will appreciate your dog's affection and enthusiastic greetings, but will your friends feel the same if your dog jumps up on them to say hello?

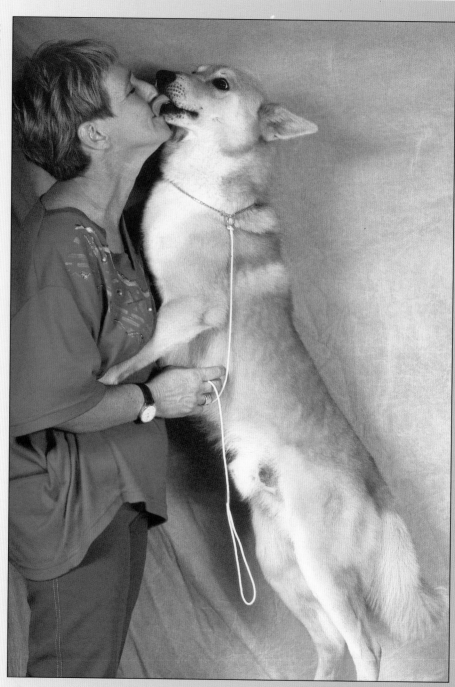

alone, but the dog needs to know that, while he can depend on you for his care, you do not have to be by his side 24 hours a day. Some behaviorists recommend tiring the dog out before you leave home—take him for a good long walk or engage in a game of fetch in the yard.

When the dog is alone in the house, he should be placed in his crate—another distinct advantage to crate training your dog. The crate should be placed in his familiar happy family area, where he normally sleeps and already feels comfortable, thereby making him feel more at ease when he is alone. Be sure to give the dog a special chew toy to enjoy while he settles into his crate.

CHEWING

The national canine pastime is chewing! Every dog loves to sink his "canines" into a tasty bone, but a dog can sink his teeth into most anything, given the chance. Dogs need to chew, to massage their gums, to make their new teeth feel better and to exercise their jaws. This is a natural behavior that is deeply embedded in all things canine. Our role as owners is not to stop the dog's chewing, but rather to redirect it to positive, chew-worthy objects. Be an informed owner and purchase proper chew toys, like strong nylon bones, that will not splinter. Be sure that the objects

are safe and durable, since your dog's safety is at risk. Again, the owner is responsible for ensuring a dog-proof environment.

The best answer is prevention; that is, put your shoes, coat and other tasty objects in their proper places (out of the reach of the growing canine mouth). Direct puppies to their toys whenever you see them "tasting" the furniture legs or the leg of a guest. Make a loud noise to attract the pup's attention and immediately escort him to his chew toy and engage him with the toy for at least four minutes, praising and encouraging him all the while. An array of safe, interesting chew toys will keep your dog's mind and teeth occupied and distracted from chewing on things he shouldn't.

Some trainers recommend deterrents, such as hot pepper, a bitter spice or a product designed for this purpose, to discourage the dog from chewing unwanted objects. Test these products to see which works best before investing in large quantities.

JUMPING UP

Jumping up is an unacceptable behavior that can become a nuisance if not corrected early on. Pick a command such as "Off" (avoid using "Down" since you will use that for the dog to lie down) and tell your Canaan "Off" when he jumps up. Place him on the ground on all fours and have him sit, praising him the whole time. Always lavish him with praise and petting when he is in the sit position. In this way, you can give him a warm affectionate greeting, let him know that you are as excited to see him as he is to see you and instill good manners at the same time!

FOOD STEALING

Is your dog devising ways of stealing food from your coffee table or kitchen counter? If so, you must answer the following questions: Is your Canaan hungry, or is he "constantly famished" like many dogs seem to be? Face it, some dogs are more food-

Teach your Canaan early on that his mealtime is at his food bowl, not at your dinner table.

motivated than others are. They are totally obsessed by the smell of food and can only think of their next meal. Food stealing is terrific fun and always yields a great reward—FOOD, glorious food.

Your goal as an owner, therefore, is to be sensible about where food is placed in the home and to reprimand your dog whenever he is caught in the act of stealing. But remember, only reprimand your dog if you actually see him stealing, not later when the crime is discovered; that will be of no use at all and will only serve to confuse him.

BEGGING

Just like food stealing, begging is a favorite pastime of hungry puppies! It achieves that same terrific result—FOOD! Dogs quickly learn that their owners keep the "good food" for themselves, and that we humans do not dine on dry food alone. Begging is a conditioned response related to a specific stimulus, time and place. The sounds of the kitchen, cans and bottles opening, crinkling bags, the smell of food in preparation, etc., will excite the dog, and soon the paws will be in the air!

Here is the solution to stopping this behavior: Never give in to a beggar! You are rewarding the dog for sitting pretty, jumping up, whining and rubbing his nose into you by giving him food. By

THE ORIGIN OF THE DINNER BELL

The study of animal behavior can be traced back to the 1800s and the renowned psychologist, Pavlov. When it was time for his dogs to eat, Pavlov would ring a bell, then feed the dogs. Pavlov soon discovered that the dogs learned to associate the bell with food and would drool at the sound of a bell. And you thought yours was the only dog obsessed with eating!

ignoring the dog, you will (eventually) force the behavior into extinction. Note that the behavior is likely to get worse before it disappears, so be sure there are not any "softies" in the family who will give in to little "Oliver" every time he whimpers, "More, please."

COPROPHAGIA

Feces eating is, to humans, one of the most disgusting behaviors that their dogs could engage in, yet, to dogs, it is perfectly normal. It is hard for us to understand why a dog would want to eat his own feces. He could be seeking certain nutrients that are missing from his diet, he could be just plain hungry or he could be attracted by the pleasing (to a dog) scent. While coprophagia most often refers to the dog's eating his own feces, a dog may just as likely eat that of another animal as well if he comes across it. Dogs often find the stool of cats and horses more palatable than that of other dogs.

Vets have found that diets with low levels of digestibility, containing relatively low levels of fiber and high levels of starch, increase coprophagia. Therefore, high-fiber diets may decrease the likelihood of dogs' eating feces. Both the consistency of the stool (how firm it feels in the dog's mouth) and the presence of undigested nutrients increase the likelihood. Once the dog develops diarrhea from feces eating, he will likely stop this distasteful habit.

To discourage this behavior, first make sure that the food you are feeding your dog is nutritionally complete and that he is getting enough food. If changes in his diet do not seem to work, and no medical cause can be found, you will have to modify the behavior through environmental control before it becomes a habit. The best way to prevent your dog from eating his stool is to make it unavailable—clean up after he eliminates and remove any stool from the yard. If it is not there, he cannot eat it.

Reprimanding for stool eating rarely impresses the dog. Vets recommend distracting the dog while he is in the act of stool eating. Coprophagia is seen most frequently in pups 6 to 12 months of age, and usually disappears around the dog's first birthday.

INDEX

My Canaan Dog

PUT YOUR PUPPY'S FIRST PICTURE HERE

Dog's Name _____

Date _____ Photographer _____